When Power and Piety Collide

When Power and Piety Collide

A Critical Analysis of Early Caliphate in Islam

Understanding the Present by Knowing the Past

Sayed Moustafa al-Qazwini

Islamic Educational Center of Orange County
3194-B Airport Loop Drive
Costa Mesa, California 92626 U.S.A.
Telephone: (714) 432-0060

www.iecoc.org
info@iecoc.org

First U.S. Edition 2009
Copyright 2009 by Moustafa al-Qazwini

The Library of Congress Cataloging-in-Publication Data
Al-Qazwini, Moustafa
When Power and Piety Collide/Moustafa al-Qazwini
p. cm.

ISBN: 978-0-9711538-0-6

Book Layout and Design by the Islamic Publishing House [www.iph.ca]
Sponsored by Ahlul Bayt Society – www.12imams.org

Printed in Canada by Friesens Corporation - www.friesens.com

Contents

When Power and Piety Collide
A Critical Analysis of Early Caliphate in Islam

Prologue

بِسْمِ اللهِ الرَّحْمَنِ الرَّحِيمِ

﴿وَإِذَا قِيلَ لَهُمُ اتَّبِعُوا مَآ أَنزَلَ اللَّهُ قَالُوا بَلْ نَتَّبِعُ مَآ أَلْفَيْنَا عَلَيْهِ آبَآءَنَآ أَوَلَوْ كَانَ آبَاؤُهُمْ لاَ يَعْقِلُونَ شَيْئًا وَلاَ يَهْتَدُونَ﴾

When it is said to them: 'Follow what Allah hath revealed,' they say: 'Nay! We shall follow the ways of our fathers.' What! Even though their fathers were void of wisdom and guidance?

Holy Qur'an, 2:170

In our present era, it is most disturbing for many Muslims and non-Muslims alike to witness the escalating rise in sectarian violence between the Shia and Sunni followers of Islam, particularly in places such as Iraq, Afghanistan, and Pakistan. Some people, including Muslims, ask why the Shia and Sunni are violently murdering each other; is there something in the history of the Muslims that continues to spark such hatred and violence today; why does one sect accuse the other of heresy; and why is one sect of the Muslims considered as "mainstream," while the other wing is branded unconventional and literally pacified?

Unquestionably, seeded in the history of Islam is the answer - in particular, the political course that was taken following the death of the

Holy Prophet and the way in which the early history of Islam was written. They say that history is bound to repeat itself and this is much more apparent today because the remnants and unconsciousness of Muslims in regards to their own history is affecting Muslims today. The account of the Muslims is *not* the classical historical case of not knowing their past, but rather, it is of not knowing the *truth* of its past. Thus, a closer examination into the past political and historical accounts of Islam is needed.

As a Muslim scholar, I get numerous questions from Muslims, both of the Shia and Sunni following (but mainly from Sunni parishioners), as to the differences between the Shia and Sunni communities. The answer does not lie in a simple stated sentence or two, but rather, it requires an honest, detailed account and interpretive explanation of the past. Hence, a truthful and comprehensive contemporary account must be told in order for sincere seekers to understand what happened to the Muslims, and why, in particular, some refer to themselves as being Shia.

Over fourteen hundred years have passed since Prophet Muhammad bonded rival tribes, united neighbors, and partnered others to form one community - the Muslim ummah. However, from the moment that Prophet Muhammad publicly declared his prophethood and message until now, the internal relationship of the Muslim ummah has yet to synthesize fully because of the Shia-Sunni division. This is not to say that there is an internal rift within Islam, far from that! Muslims are united in the same God, they recite the same Holy Qur'an, face the same *qiblah* (direction of prayer), fast the same month (of Ramadhan), and perform the pilgrimage to the same House (Ka'abah).

Nonetheless, there is a domestic struggle and this strain is embedded in the historical and political account of Islam; in particular, the caliphates[1] of Abu Bakr,[2] Umar b. al-Khattab,[3] and Uthman b. al-Affan.[4]

---

[1] Caliph (caliphs) is the person intended to be the successor (leader) to Prophet Muhammad.

For many Muslims, the first three caliphs are highly revered and the unquestioning belief in the righteousness of them as the "rightly guided" caliphs lies at the heart of many Muslims' faith. Nonetheless, the stark realization that these caliphs made severe misjudgments may surprise some, perhaps even bewilder or shatter their belief. Uncovering the truthful facts of the first three caliphs may seem disrespectful for some; however, this is actually a respectful attempt to restore Islam to its pristine, original form brought by Prophet Muhammad.

As difficult as it may be, we (Muslims) must be able to objectively examine the history of these three caliphs, re-examine and filter out our hadith sources, and then make sound judgment based on facts.

Since the "split" of the Muslims (Shia and Sunni) can be summoned to have intensified during the administration of the first three caliphs, and much of today's estrangement of the Muslims can be traced back to their government, consequently, this book will outline the character, actions, qualifications, and consequences of these three individuals. The reports are based solely on the historical accounts of Sunni sources, such as the respected texts: *Sahih al-Bukhari* and *Sahih al-Muslim,* and other renowned Sunni scholars. Thus, no claim can be argued that the author is vindictively judging the three caliphs from outside sources.

---

[2] (Abu Bakr) Abdullah b. Abi Quhafah, his mother is Salma b. Shakher. He is the father of Aishah, the wife of the Prophet. He was born fifty-one years before the Hijrah; died on the 22nd Jumadi al-Awwal, 13 AH and assumed the caliphate after the Prophet's death for a period of two years and four months.

[3] Umar b. al-Khattab was born forty years before the Hijrah. He accepted Islam six years after the advent of Islam and was appointed by Abu Bakr to be the second successor to the Prophet and reined for ten years. He was assassinated in 23 AH in Madinah. He appointed Mu'awiyah b. Abu Sufyan as the governor of Damascus.

[4] Uthman b. al-Affan was chosen by Umar to be in the group of six candidates for succession. His tribe, Bani Umayyah, swept and dominated important political and military leadership. He assumed the caliphate in 23 AH and during his reign, the *"fitna kubra"* (great mischief) occurred. He was killed in his home by revolutionist in 35 AH in Madinah.

Furthermore, the readings will also cover the view of the Shia and shed some light as to why the Shia have been marginalized throughout the Muslim history.

As a scholar of Islam and a member of the Muslim ummah, this writing is not intended to be derogatory, or as an attempt to maliciously blame some, or as a means to jostle the past of the Muslims; nor is it an opportunity by the author to insult or expose the weaknesses of some companions. Rather this work is an attempt to shed light and present an unbiased account of their actions and the subsequent results on the ummah, such as their plans to dominate the Muslim leadership, the need to develop the science of Hadith (Prophetic traditions), discordant ideological interpretations, and the emergence of the schools of thought. Furthermore, this work is not meant to stir sectarian conflict or to cause a deeper fissure amongst the schools either. I am well aware and sensitive to the fact that this is a delicate issue and I take to practice every means possible to express my sentiments and academic knowledge respectfully and rationally.

Throughout the years of humbly serving my faith, I have maintained an open venue to foster intrafaith engagements and reconciliation. The time has come for Muslim scholars to set aside their differences and rise to the occasion and challenges by addressing their internal division in an honest, academic, and composed fashion. All provocations and polemics must desist on both fronts and a deep knowledge of being acquainted first-hand about each other's history, ideology, and stance are critical ingredients for any plausible discussions or solutions to arise.

For many years, it has been rumored that the Shia do not favor the companions of the Prophet; however, the reality is that the Shia have always revered, respected, and acknowledged many of the companions. Over 100,000 companions lived during the time of the Prophet - most were sincere, but not all of them and even the Holy Qur'an attest to this (al-Qur'an, c. 63[5] & c. 9:101[6]). We recognize and pay tribute to those who sincerely serviced, sacrificed, and gave their lives for the sake of Islam and the Prophet.[7] The Shia are highly recognized for paying their respect to many companions of the Prophet who were martyred to advance Islam. We make yearly pilgrimages to their places of burial - their mausoleums and even to the battlegrounds where they lost their lives. Despite the love we have for the faithful martyrs of Islam, still we are continuously branded as those who dislike the companions.

The Shia have primarily been the most misunderstood of the Muslim schools of thought. It has been the case throughout Muslim history and until now that the Shia ideology and its followers are persecuted and ridiculed. In recent times, it is been more accelerated politically after the invasion of Iraq in 2003. The Muslim world then witnessed an increasing attack against Shia Islam and its followers. A tsunami effect of ignorance and prejudice batters the Shia. Unsubstantially described as "interpreting their own form of Islam," the Shia have been hammered with radical accusations as being "renegades" and "rebellious" by those who believe that the Shia doctrine is some form of a "cult" or that it is at "odds" with mainstream Muslims.

Some known and well-respected Sunni scholars, from the past until the present, have from time to time labeled the Shia followers as "innovators," some even going as far as calling them "heretics." Such labeled biases spread doubt and fear amongst the ummah, and even

---

[5] *Holy Qur'an*, 63:1, "When the hypocrites come to you they say, 'We bear witness that you are indeed the apostle of God.' God knows that you are indeed His Apostle, and God bears witness that the hypocrites are indeed liars."

[6] *Holy Qur'an*, 9:101, "Round about you [Muhammad and his community] and among you in Madinah are hypocrites and they are obstinate in hypocrisy. You do not know them, We know them, twice shall We punish them and in addition shall be sent to a grievous penalty."

[7] *Holy Qur'an*, 9:100, "And as to the foremost from among the Muhajireen (Immigrants) and Ansar (Helpers) and those who followed them in goodness, Allah is well pleased with them and they are well pleased with Him..."

worse, mistrust. What is more is that intellectual and moderate Muslim leaders have largely ignored the incredulous accusations and labeling. The silence by those religious leaders has engendered more ignorance and division amongst the Shia-Sunni schools and their followers.

The fallacy about Shia Islam needs to end and this is where my duty and obligation lies, for Allah says in the Holy Qur'an, "To make it known and clear to mankind and not to hide it." (c. 3:187) I stand to defend any dehumanizing portrayal of the Shia by adversaries, and it is my duty to expunge the rumors that have beleaguered us (Shia) for many centuries.

An honest and unabashed work is far overdue on this subject. I have no secret agenda, nor the need to practice the license of *taqiyyah*,[8] and I stand free of any association to proselytize the Shia school of thought. These are far from my objective; rather, my aim is to put forward the historical truth objectively about what some of the companions did systematically during the life of the Prophet and following his death, and to allow the reader to make his or her own sound conclusion.

Every Muslim, in fact, every human being bears the moral responsibility of seeking out the truth. For those who are sincerely searching for the truth, they must put aside any personal opinion and approach this work without pretense or prejudice views.

Although the history of Islam has hitherto led a tenuous path, the damage is not irreparable, for Allah says in the Noble Qur'an (c. 13:11), "Allah does not change the condition of the people until they change what is within them."

The Muslims have freedom of choice and the Muslims still have the opportunity to liberate themselves and go forward as an ummah, united in submission to Allah.

---

[8] *Taqiyyah* is a form of concealment of one's belief in order to protect one's life, property, family, etc.

I welcome any contributing comments provided they are based and structured academically and rationally, mutually accepted amongst the various Muslim scholars, and free of personal rhetoric.

Sayed Moustafa al-Qazwini
January 2009
Muharram 1430
Orange County, California
USA

Acknowledgement

This publication of this book would not have been possible without the effort, sacrifice, and sincere dedication of a few people that the Almighty has graced me with.

First, my gratitude must be expressed to Sister Fatma Saleh, her imprint on this book is unspoken. Second, much appreciation goes to Shaykh Saleem Bhimji for the typesetting and cover design; and his wife, Sister Arifa Hudda for the editing of this work. Publication of this book was made possible by the Ahlul Bayt Society (www.12imams.com).

Dedication

This book is dedicated to my honorable father and mother. My father who taught me the ways of Islam, in its humbleness and reasoning, and nurtured me in the love for Allah, *Glorified and Exalted is He*, the Prophet, and his immaculate Household. Moreover, for my mother, for her unconditional love and patience in raising me into the person that I am today. To them both I am eternally grateful.

It is customary in Islam that when the name of Allah, Prophet Muhammad, the other prophets, or imams (descendants and successors of Prophet Muhammad) is enunciated, the following phrases are mentioned:

Allah - *"Glorified and Exalted is He"* (Subhannah wa-tallah).

Prophet Muhammad - *"Peace be upon him and his family."*

After the names of prophets, imams from the family of Prophet Muhammad and his daughter - *"Peace be upon him/her."*

With great respect, admiration, recognition, and praise, I have omitted the mentioned phrases for the sake of continuity.

Chapter 1
Smashing the Idols of Tribalism

﴿وَجَعَلُوا لِلَّهِ أَندَاداً لِّيُضِلُّوا عَنْ سَبِيلِهِ قُلْ تَمَتَّعُوا فَإِنَّ
مَصِيرَكُمْ إِلَى ٱلنَّارِ﴾

And they set up (idols) as equal to Allah, to mislead (men) from His Path! Say, 'Enjoy [for a while], for indeed your destination is towards the Fire!'

Holy Qur'an, 14:30

As befits the final Messenger of Allah, Prophet Muhammad was born into the noblest Arab family of his region, the tribe of Bani Hashim in Arabia, in the sixth century. His prestigious lineage stretched back to Prophet Ibrahim, and his ancestors distinguished themselves through integrity, (belief in) monotheism, and bravery. His virtues were visible amongst the Quraysh tribes who entitled him as "Muhammad, the Truthful and the Trustworthy One (As-Sadiq al-Ameen)." When Allah called upon Prophet Muhammad to publicly declare his prophethood, these virtues assisted him to bring forth the message of Islam.

For that environment, the revolutionary message of Islam shattered tribal, ethnic, and imperial barriers. In a society where ancestry dictated respect and exclusiveness, the Prophet proclaimed the opposite, he said, "Anyone who has an atom's weight of prejudice in his heart will not enter Paradise."[1] In stark contrast to the highly stratified society to which Islam came, the Prophet paralleled the rich with the poor, the

---

[1] Al-Kulayni, *Al-Kafi*, Vol. 2; *Bab al-Asabiyah*, p. 308, hadith 3

desert nomads with the urban dwellers, and the rulers with the ruled, side by side in prayer to Allah at the Holy Ka'abah. Their monotheism came at a time when the Ka'abah, initially reconstructed by Prophet Ibrahim had been usurped for idol worshipping, and members of the Prophet's extended tribe, the Quraysh relied upon the revenue from the pilgrims who flocked to the House of Idols. Needless to say, the majority of the Quraysh were less than pleased with the idea of destroying the statues and lucrative income for the sake of restoring the foundation of monotheism.

Understandably then, despite his noble roots, the tribal relation with the Prophet became chafe as he rapidly spread the messages of unity, equality, and monotheism. Accustomed to their status as the highest of the high, the Quraysh were less than thrilled with the proclamation from God that read:

﴿يَا أَيُّهَا ٱلنَّاسُ إِنَّا خَلَقْنَاكُم مِّن ذَكَرٍ وَأُنثَىٰ وَجَعَلْنَاكُمْ شُعُوباً وَقَبَائِلَ لِتَعَارَفُوا إِنَّ أَكْرَمَكُمْ عِندَ ٱللَّهِ أَتْقَاكُمْ إِنَّ ٱللَّهَ عَلِيمٌ خَبِيرٌ﴾

O Mankind! We created you from a male and a female and then made you into nations and tribes only that you might recognize each other; verily, the most honored of you before Allah is the most righteous. (c. 49:13)

While the sincere people, such as the Prophet's cousin, Ali b. Abi Talib, the Prophet's wife, Khadijah b. Khuwaylid, Ali's father who was also the uncle of the Prophet, Abu Talib, and the Prophet's uncle, Hamzah b. Abdul Muttalib immediately recognized the truth and devoted their lives to it, the majority of the Prophet's tribe (Quraysh) threw all of their might and fury against the Prophet. War, sanctions, murder, and exile were the welcome that they gave their kinsman in return for his dedication towards Allah and for many years, they proved to be the staunchest enemies of Islam.

Since the early Muslims were few, the Quraysh were secure in their ridicule of the Prophet, whom they considered as an insane maniac. However, Allah states otherwise, "And you are not, by the grace of your Lord, possessed." (c. 68:2) However, his movement progressed from a diminutive posture to a fast growing threat against the powerful figures of the Quraysh. Increasingly, the Prophet and his mounting followers became incessantly persecuted. The Prophet saw no choice but to leave his beloved birthplace of Mecca and take up the invitation by the people of Madinah[2] to foster Islam.

The move to Madinah became a decisive maneuver. Nothing could have aided Islam more because the inhabitants of Madinah were ready and willing to join the cause of Islam and bring forth Islam from the inner-personal to the public sphere. Even military oppositions by the Quraysh could not stop the exploding spread of the message of Islam. After nine years of exile, at the command of Allah, the Muslims were prepared to retake the seat of monotheism and restore Mecca to the rule of the Prophet, rather than the rule of idolaters.

Even after the final conquest of Mecca by the Muslims, most of the Quraysh still vehemently opposed the message of Islam. Thus, two options faced those who opposed Islam - either merge with the Muslims or become marginalized. Many of the harshest enemies of Islam who had hitherto, at the least, thrown trash and stones at the Holy Prophet, artificially converted to Islam. Swiftly some of his formidable foes became his closest companions. Commanders who had staunchly fought against him for many years now feigned to his side, such as Abu Sufyan from the clan of the Bani Umayyah and Khalid b. al-Waleed. Since they

---

[2] The original name of Madinah was Yathrib, but it later became known as Madinatul Nabi (the City of the Prophet) after the migration (Hijrah) of the Prophet from Mecca to Madinah.

could not defeat the Prophet, his enemies saw no other choice but to superficially join him.

Undoubtedly, many of these conversions were sincere and the Qur'an testifies to this, "And as to the foremost from among the Muhajireen (Immigrants from Mecca) and Ansar (Helpers from Madinah) and those who followed them in goodness, Allah is well pleased with them and they are well pleased with Him..." (c. 9:100) In fact, Muslims today owe a great deal of gratitude to those who initially fought for and supported Islam. Their sacrifices led to the success of Islam's survival and continuous drive. Nonetheless, as evinced by *Surah al-Munafiqun (The Hypocrites* - c. 63) and *Surah al-Taubah (The Repentance* - c. 9) faith did not enter all of their hearts:

﴿إِذَا جَاءَكَ الْمُنَافِقُونَ قَالُوا نَشْهَدُ إِنَّكَ لَرَسُولُ اللَّهِ وَاللَّهُ يَعْلَمُ إِنَّكَ لَرَسُولُهُ وَاللَّهُ يَشْهَدُ إِنَّ الْمُنَافِقِينَ لَكَاذِبُونَ﴾

When the hypocrites come to you, they say, 'We bear witness that you are indeed the Messenger of Allah.' Surely, Allah knows that you are indeed His messenger, and Allah bears witness that the hypocrites are indeed liars. (c. 63:1)

﴿وَمِمَّنْ حَوْلَكُم مِّنَ الْأَعْرَابِ مُنَافِقُونَ وَمِنْ أَهْلِ الْمَدِينَةِ مَرَدُوا عَلَى النِّفَاقِ لَا تَعْلَمُهُمْ نَحْنُ نَعْلَمُهُمْ سَنُعَذِّبُهُم مَّرَّتَيْنِ ثُمَّ يُرَدُّونَ إِلَىٰ عَذَابٍ عَظِيمٍ﴾

Round about you [Muhammad and his community] and among you in Madinah are hypocrites and they are obstinate in hypocrisy. You do not know them, We know them, twice shall We punish them and in addition they shall be sent to a grievous penalty. (c. 9:101)

4

Chapter 2
Quraysh Group

﴿مَّا أَصَابَكَ مِنْ حَسَنَةٍ فَمِنَ اللهِ وَمَا أَصَابَكَ مِن سَيِّئَةٍ فَمِنْ
نَفْسِكَ وَأَرْسَلْنَاكَ لِلنَّاسِ رَسُولاً وَكَفَى بِاللهِ شَهِيدًا﴾

*Whatever good happens to you is from Allah. But whatever evil
(calamities) happens to you is from your (own) soul. And We have
sent you as an apostle to (instruct) humankind. And enough is
Allah as a witness.*

Holy Qur'an, 4:79

Development of the Quraysh Group

While some of the Quraysh truly believed in and supported the message
of Islam and the Messenger of God without any self-ambition, others
also believed but aspired for more. They saw an opportunity on the
horizon for future power and that path was through political means.
Thus, a group formed that consisted of several companions who
belonged mainly to the Quraysh tribe. Amongst those who were at the
forefront of this power group were some of the most prominent
companions, such as Abu Bakr Abdullah b. Abi Quhafah, Umar b. al-
Khattab, Uthman b. al-Affan, Al-Mugheerah b. Shu'bah, Abu Musa al-
Ashari, Salim Mawla Abi Hudayfah, Husayd b. Hudayr, Basheer b. Sa'd,
Muhammad b. Muslim, Ma'adh b. Jabal, and Zayd b. Thabit.

This Quraysh group began its development at a time when the
Prophet was setting roots in Madinah. In the span of a few years, the
Prophet had revolutionized, empowered, and united dissident tribes to
form an Islamic nation. His word was the word of God and the faithful

flocked to his calling. All the same, he was still a mortal human being whose mortal life would eventually come to an end. The Quraysh group, who sought future ambition, knew that their power was limited, that is as long as the Prophet was alive. Aware that the Prophet was mortal, hence they bided their time and craftily considered the future structure of the Muslim leadership that would come after the death of the Prophet and what their role would be.

Objective of the Quraysh Group

Having lost their past influence as the keepers to the House of Idols, the Quraysh group foresaw an even greater opportunity to master an entire nation and its sizable wealth upon the death of the Prophet. Thus, they patiently waited to seize control of the leadership after the death of the Prophet, and they succeeded in their plans, for they held the first three caliphates and spawned the first Muslim dynasty - the Bani Umayyah.

Consequently, this group resolved to complete rule of the Muslim ummah to be in their hands. They might have begun some internal conflicts had some not agreed amongst themselves to allow three subdivisions of the Quraysh to hold power successively: the tribe of Taym, the tribe of Uday, and the tribe of Fihr. Initially, they planned to first allow Abu Bakr to represent his tribe of Taym; then Umar b. al-Khattab would represent his tribe of Uday, and then Abu Ubaydah b. al-Jarrah would represent his tribe of Fihr; however, as it happened, Uthman b. al-Affan (from the Umayyah tribe) later replaced Abu Ubaydah b. al-Jarrah. Finally, after the tribe of Fihr had completed its turn, the tribe of Taym would then take control again and the cycle would continue. They felt that this rotating agreement would ensure harmony within the Quraysh group and preserve the stability of their order.

However, the group excluded one vital section of Quraysh, namely the Bani Hashim tribe, the one to which the Prophet belonged. They did so overtly, under the pretext that Bani Hashim was already too powerful since the Prophet sprang from them. As Umar b. al-Khattab explained,

"The reason we did not want Bani Hashim to assume power after the death of the Prophet was that Quraysh disliked seeing both prophethood and leadership (*imamah*) vested in the family of Bani Hashim."[1] This is precisely where the start of the problem began for Muslims. Initially it did not stem from Islamic ideology, or interpretation of the revelations, or the *sunnah*, but rather, from the old Arab rivalry that was deeply entrenched and seeded into the jealous veins of some of the branches of the Quraysh tribes. Just as Umar b. al-Khattab said, they "disliked" seeing another family invested with so much interest.

Emergence of the Quraysh Group

During the early developing stages of the Islamic state, the Quraysh group had yet to crystallize. It was not until the departure of the Holy Prophet that the group fully emerged onto the scene. Two factors hastened its assembly and emergence: the first was the news of the Prophet's impending death; and second was the Prophet's repeated orders that Ali b. Abi Talib was to succeed him in leading the Muslim ummah.[2]

In the tenth year of the Hijrah (632 CE), the day came when the Prophet stunned the ummah by indicating that he would soon leave the world while returning from his first and last pilgrimage, forever known as the "Farewell Pilgrimage." Surrounded by over 100,000 *hujjaj* (pilgrims) in the blazing heat, near the oasis pond of Ghadir Khum,[3] the Prophet was intercepted with a revelation that forced him to stop the pilgrims in their track to hear a new revelation from Allah. The revelation was as follows:

---

[1] Ibn al-Atheer, *Al-Kamil fil-Tarikh*, 3:24; Al-Tabari, *Tarikh al-Tabari*, 2:223

[2] Successorship (*khalifah* or *imamah*) according to both schools of thought, Ahlul Bayt and Companions, is the representation of Prophet Muhammad, in the affairs of *deen* (faith) and *duniyah* (life).

[3] Ghadir Khum (which is close to today's al-Juhfah in the Arabian Peninsula). It was the center point where routes from different provinces met and then parted to go their separate ways.

﴿يَا أَيُّهَا الرَّسُولُ بَلِّغْ مَا أُنْزِلَ إِلَيْكَ مِنْ رَبِّكَ وَإِنْ لَمْ تَفْعَلْ فَمَا بَلَّغْتَ رِسَالَتَهُ وَاللّهُ يَعْصِمُكَ مِنَ النَّاسِ إِنَّ اللّهَ لاَ يَهْدِي الْقَوْمَ الْكَافِرِينَ﴾

O Messenger! Convey what had been revealed to you from your Lord; if you do not do so, then [it would be as if] you have not conveyed His message [at all]. Allah will protect you from the people. (c. 5:67)

After revealing this verse, the Prophet then gave his famous last sermon known as *Khutbatul Widah* (The Farewell Sermon).

After praising God, the Prophet openly spoke to the pilgrims that the Angel Gabriel had reviewed the Holy Qur'an with him twice that year instead of once, and this was a sign that his time of death was near.[4]

Then the critical question was at hand, the Prophet asked the pilgrims if he had more authority (*wilayah*) over the believers than they had over themselves, to which they all replied, "yes." Then the Prophet raised the hand of Ali b. Abi Talib and said, "Whosoever's master (*mawla*) I am, this Ali is also his master (*man kuntu mawlahu fa hadha Aliyun mawlahu*)." The order was sealed and Ali b. Abi Talib became the Prophet's successor by Divine order. At this point, the Prophet publicly took the oaths from those present, including Abu Bakr, Umar b. al-Khattab,[5] Ammar b. Yasir, Abu Dharr al-Ghifari, Salman al-Farsi, al-Miqdaad b. al-Aswad, and Abdullah b. al-Abbas. Some even approached Ali to congratulate him personally, like Umar b. al-Khattab, who said,

---

[4] Al-Tabari, *Tarikh al-Tabari*, 2:435

[5] Ahmad b. Hanbal, *Musnad Ahmad*, 4:281; *Sirr al-Alamin*; Al-Tabari, *Al-Riyadh al-Nadhirah*, 2:169

"Congratulations Ibn Abi Talib! Today you became the leader (*mawla*) of all believing men and women."[6]

An excerpt of the Prophet's farewell sermon:

> It is probable that I will be called soon and I will respond. So I leave behind me among you two weighty [very worthy and important] things: the Book of Allah, which is a rope stretched between the heavens and the Earth; and my progeny [Ahlul Bayt]. For verily Allah, the Merciful, the Aware informed me that these two would never become separated from each other until they meet at the Fount of Abundance.[7] Therefore, be careful how you will treat these two in my absence.

This was not the first time that the Holy Prophet had named Ali b. Abi Talib as his successor (aside from referring to the designated members of his Ahlul Bayt that were to succeed him) on numerous occasions, such as in the "Feast of the Clan" (*al-Indhar*).[8] Moreover, portions of the Holy Qur'an refer to Ali b. Talib's successionship.[9]

---

[6] Ahmad b. Hanbal, *Musnad Ahmad* 4:81, Ibn Abu Yallah al-Musilli, *Musnad*; Abu Bakr b. Abi Shibah, *Al-Musnaf*; Abu Bakr al-Baghdadi; *Sirr al-Alamin*, Abu Hamid al-Ghazali; *Al-Milal wal-Nihal*, Abu al-Fattah al-Shahrestani; *Al-Bidayah wa al-Nihaya*, 5:209; Ibn Katheer al-Shami; *Al-Sawaeq al-Muhriqah*, Ibn Hajar al-Askalani, p.26; *Tafseer al-Tabari*, 3:310; Muhammad b. Jarrer, Allamah Amini in *Al-Ghadeer*, 1:283, has compiled over sixty prominent Sunni sources that narrated the congratulations of Abu Bakr and Umar to Imam Ali on his succession by the Prophet on the Day of Ghadir.

[7] See *Holy Qur'an*, 108:1-3

[8] "Feast of the Clan," after the revelation of c. 26:214 ("And warn thy nearest relations"), the Prophet made a feast and invited his extended family, so he could announce his prophethood and invite them to embrace his message. It was also the same event, in which the Prophet first declared that Ali b. Abi Talib would be his successor and caliph after him.

[9] See *Holy Qur'an*, 5:55 and 4:59

Quraysh Group Appears on the Scene

Prior to the Prophet's departure, the Quraysh group had been quiescent. The time was nearing and they sensed it. The first wave of the emergence began when the group distinguished itself from the population by refusing the Prophet's orders to join the dispatch of Usama b. Zayd to combat the Romans, which was one of the last military maneuvers during the Prophet's lifetime.

Although critically ill and approaching his final days, the Prophet repeatedly ordered them to join the dispatch of Usama, but they (the first three-caliphs and other companions who were present) declined to do so. Sensing that the Prophet would soon depart, the elite members of the group wanted to be in Madinah for the moment of the Prophet's death in order to assume power, quite possibly, the precise reason why the Prophet wanted them to be away. The situation escalated to the point where the Prophet strongly warned them by saying, "May the curse of Allah be upon the one who stays behind and does not join the army of Usama."[10] Aside from that, they still refused and the imminent time of the death of the Prophet was drawing near.

"Calamity of Thursday"

Three days later, after refusing to join the dispatch of Usama, was when that mournful day came and the Quraysh group was ready. As the Prophet was on his deathbed, they made their most decisive move that would ensure their transitory success - a shift that would eventually divert the course of Islamic history forever. This act later became known as the "Calamity of Thursday." This event is recorded in *Sahih al-Bukhari*, which is considered to be the most authentic book after the Holy Qur'an in the Sunni tradition.

Gravely ill, and surrounded by some of the companions, the Prophet requested a pen and paper to narrate his will, a hadith he said that

---

[10] Shahristani, *Al-Milal wal-Nihal*, 1:29

would guard the nation from misguidance.[11] Sensing that the Prophet again wanted to name his successor (Ali b. Abi Talib) one last time, the companion, Umar b. al-Khattab spearheaded the Quraysh group by interceding and declaring, "We have the book of Allah, and it suffices for us." He then accused the Prophet of Islam of hallucinating (*yahjor*) because of his illness.[12] An argument ensued over Umar's comment and the Prophet angrily requested them to leave.[13 & 14]

The power ambition was too much to let pass, because long afterwards and during his reign, Umar b. al-Khattab said regarding that day, "I knew the Prophet was going to mention the name of Ali as his successor, so I objected to that and refused."[15]

After challenging the will of the Prophet, it is not surprising to witness centuries of unsettling political and ideological differences within the ummah. Perhaps, during the eras of the first four caliphs, Islam was still a spiritually inclined faith and united and bonded by primarily one following - one ummah - but the aspirations of some permitted the way of division. The institute of the *khalifah* was reduced to a mere political acquisition and many Muslims began their slow turn away from what Islam had intended. Corruption and greed earmarked the powerhouses of government and institutes that later sprung up during the Bani Umayyah and Bani Abbas dynasties. It can be said that

---

[11] The Messenger of God said, "Bring me a tablet (*lawh*) and an inkpot (*dawat*), so that I can write for you a document, after which you will not go astray." A person said that the Messenger of God was talking "deliriously." *Tarikh al-Tabari*, Vol. 9 translated by Ismail. K. Poonawala p. 175.

[12] In the older *Sahih al-Bukhari* books, the term "*yahjor*" can be found, but in the latest versions, the hadith has been modified as, "that the Prophet has been overwhelmed by pain."

[13] *Sahih al-Bukhari, Kitab al-Jihad wal-Seer*, 2:118; *Sahih al-Muslim; Ithbat al-Wasyah; Musnad Ahmad*, 3:346

[14] For full details read *Inquiries about Shia Islam* by the same author.

[15] Ibn Abil Hadid, *Sharh Nahjul-Balaghah*, 3:114

the era of corruption by these dynasties had been intricately connected to the "Calamity of Thursday."

Chapter 3
The Saqifah Union

﴿وَمَا مُحَمَّدٌ إِلَّا رَسُولٌ قَدْ خَلَتْ مِن قَبْلِهِ الرُّسُلُ أَفَإِنْ مَّاتَ
أَوْ قُتِلَ إِنقَلَبْتُمْ عَلَى أَعْقَابِكُمْ وَمَن يَنقَلِبْ عَلَى عَقِبَيْهِ فَلَن
يَضُرَّ اللَّهَ شَيْئًا وَسَيَجْزِي اللَّهُ الشَّاكِرِينَ﴾

*Muhammad is no more than an apostle: many were the apostle that
passed away before him. If he died or was slain, will you then turn
back on your heels? If any did turn back on his heels, not the least
harm will he do to Allah. But Allah (on the other hand) will swiftly
reward those who (serve Him) with gratitude.*

Holy Qur'an, 3:144

Having faced hostile aggression, economic boycott and expulsion, an
invitation was extended to the Prophet and his followers to uproot
themselves from their homeland and migrate to the desert oasis of
Yathrib (which was later renamed Madinah). The invitation came from
the Ansar (Helpers) who were the inhabitants of Madinah.[1] In the year
622 CE, the Prophet and the Muhajireen[2] arrived in Madinah and along

---

[1] The Ansar (the Helpers) consisted of two tribes, the Aws and the Khazraj who lived in
the oasis desert of Yathrib which is about 250 miles northeast of Mecca. These two tribes
had been at bitter and deadly odds with each other for many years and with the
Prophet's assistance, they put aside their differences and invited the Prophet and his
followers to Yathrib, which was later renamed Madinah.

[2] Those who migrated with the Prophet from Mecca to Madinah are known as the
Muhajireen - a term that means someone who is fleeing. The Muhajireen were the
indigenous inhabitants of Mecca, mainly from the tribe of Quraysh.

with the Ansar, they established the first official Muslim state.

Chronicles of Saqifah

On the 28th of Safar, 632 CE (11 AH), four days after the "Calamity of Thursday" occurred, Prophet Muhammad, the Seal of the Messengers passed away. The believing men, women, and children wandered in shock as if one of their own family members had died. At the same time, a select few were anxious to gain power. They knew that they could not simply declare themselves as the new guardians of the ummah because the Prophet had already explicitly declared Ali b. Abi Talib as his successor. Had they done so, even though the Muslims were still in a state of grief, they would have rejected them and their authority. Thus, they took a much more subtle approach.

As the Prophet's body lay in wait, Ali b. Abi Talib and the immediate family of the Bani Hashim were busy preparing the Prophet's body for burial. With the family of the Prophet being preoccupied, several members of the Ansar tribe arranged for a private meeting far away from the Prophet's mosque at a place called Saqifah Bani Sa'idah. They had grown concerned about the leadership (*khalifah*) of the ummah and wanted to ensure a smooth transition of Ali b. Abi Talib's office post.

Despite having welcomed the Muhajireen into their town, the Ansar had all along been fearful and cautious of their domination in Madinah; even more, they were fearful of the power their relatives maintained in Mecca. Concerned that the Muhajireen might make the initial move to secure leadership of the ummah, the Ansar took a pre-emptive measure to discuss and uphold their support of Ali b. Abi Talib. This was their initial plan; however, the meeting took a turn. Some members of the Ansar sensed that the leadership was going to slip away from Ali b. Abi Talib, hence they began to discuss the seizing of leadership for themselves.

Large in numbers and a formidable tribe to contend with, some of them felt that the Ansar had rights for leadership since they were the ones who had fully participated in the battles of Badr, Uhud, Khaybar, and Hunayn, as well as the two "Bayahs of Ridhwan."[3] In addition, the Holy Prophet had stated the following about the Ansar, "Only a believer loves the Ansar, and only a hypocrite dislikes them."[4] Moreover, they were quite familiar with the old rivalry of the Quraysh tribe.

Envy and blood feud, although dormant, was deeply felt amongst the Quraysh tribe. In particular, their jealousy was directed against Ali b. Abi Talib for numerous reasons - including the fact that he stood as a stark reminder about the lives of the members of the Quraysh that he took away in defending Islam in the various battles.

In one battle alone, Ali b. Abi Talib took the lives of seventy elite members of the Quraysh. This was ingrained too deep into the memory of those Quraysh families to ignore and no matter how much they embraced Islam, the loss of their family members was far greater for

---

[3] The Pledge of Ridhwan: In Dhul-Qa'dah, 6 AH, the Prophet decided to perform the *umrah* (the lesser pilgrimage) to the Ka'abah which had been until then denied to the Muslims due to the hostility of the Meccans. Fourteen hundred Muhajireen and Ansar showed readiness to go with him. Lest there be any misgivings in any quarter about his intentions, he directed the Muslims not to carry any arms other than swords, and he himself put on the robes of *ihram* and took camels to sacrifice. The Muslims camped at Hudaibiyah, ten miles from Mecca. An envoy was sent to the Meccans to obtain their permission for visiting the Ka'abah but it was rejected. Instead, the Meccans collected a force to prevent the Muslims from entering Mecca. The Quraysh sent Budayl of the tribe of Khuza'ah, to tell the Prophet that he was not allowed to visit the Ka'abah. The Prophet said that he had not gone there to fight but to perform the pilgrimage. The Quraysh deputed 'Urwah ibn Mas'ud al-Thaqafi to have a talk with the Prophet, but nothing came out of it. The Prophet then sent Karash ibn Umayyah to the Quraysh, but the messenger was mistreated, and it was only with difficulty that he escaped without being killed. The vanguard of the Quraysh attacked the Muslims, but it was captured. The Prophet demonstrated great clemency and set the captives free. Ultimately, Uthman (who belonged to the same clan in which Abu Sufyan belonged) was sent to persuade the Quraysh to allow the Muslims to visit the Ka'abah. News came that the Quraysh had killed Uthman. The Muslims took a pledge on the hands of the Prophet, known as "Bay'at al-Ridhwan" to stand by him to the last. Referring to this pledge, the Qur'an says: *Indeed God was well pleased with the believers when they swore allegiance to thee under the tree, and He knew what was in their hearts, so He sent down tranquility on them and rewarded them with a near victory.* (c. 48:18)

[4] *Sahih al-Muslim*, 1:33, hadith 75

some or too fresh in their memories to forget. The Ansar were quite familiar with this, but on the other hand, they did not have to contend with such animosity and rivalry - they had no loss of relatives that could be traced back to Ali b. Abi Talib's valor and they had no township quarrels with the Quraysh tribe.

The shaded area of Saqifah belonged to Bani Sa'idah b. Ka'ab b. al-Khazraj from the tribe of Khazraj (from the Ansar of Madinah). The meeting location was not accidental, for it was there that the Khazraj, led by Sa'd b. Ibadah used to gather underneath the shaded canopy to legislate and resolve town matters.

That day, both tribes of the Ansar - the Khazraj and Aws were present at the meeting. At the beginning of the meeting, the following were in attendance: Sa'd b. Ibadah, Ibn al-Aas, Anas b. Malik, al-Mugheerah b. Shu'bah, Khalid b. al-Waleed, Abd al-Rahman b. Auf, Basheer b. Sa'd, Ma'adh b. Jabal, and Usayd b. Hudayr.[5] Other individuals from the Muhajireen who found out about the meeting came later, such as Abu Bakr, Umar b. al-Khattab, and Abu Ubaydah b. al-Jarrah.

At the meeting, the Ansar initially recruited Sa'd b. Ibadah for the leadership of the Muslim community, however on that day he was extremely ill to the point that he could barely speak or move.[6] He was the only man other than Ali b. Abi Talib that the Quraysh group feared during the time of the Holy Prophet. Sa'd b. Ibadah was also popular amongst the Muslims - both the Muhajireen and the Ansar, due to the fact that during the battles he used to carry the flag of Islam until combat started, at which point he would pass it over to Ali b. Abi Talib.[7] However, not everyone at the meeting agreed to his nomination. Some of those present began to bicker, hence the old rivalry between the two tribes surfaced. When they realized that a mutual consensus would not

---

[5] *Tarikh al-Ya'qubi*, 2:123; Ibn Hajar, *Al-Isabah*, 1:325

[6] *Tarikh al-Tabari*, 2:455

[7] *Usud al-Ghabah*, 4:20; *Ansab al-Ashraf*, 2:106

be reached, they resounded to the following statement, "We will never pay allegiance (to anyone) except to Ali b. Abi Talib."[8]

As the tension grew at the meeting, two members from the Aws tribe, Awaim b. Sa'ad and Maen b. Obed left the meeting unnoticed. Fearing that the leadership of the Muslim community would fall into the hands of their former rivals, the Khazraj, they sought to inform Umar b. al-Khattab about what was taking place.[9]

After the two men informed Umar b. al-Khattab about the private meeting, Umar grew anxiously impatient. As it so happened, Umar had intended for Abu Bakr to be present when the death of the Holy Prophet would occur, but Abu Bakr was away in an outlying area of Madinah called al-Samh. Hence, as the news of the Prophet's death began to spread quickly and the shock and sadness amongst the Muslims grew, Umar needed to react in order to buy some time to join the meeting - and there were two reasons for this. First, Umar needed Abu Bakr to return so that both of them could attend the private meeting at Saqifah; and the other reason was to act as if the Prophet was not dead in order to delay the official appointment of Ali b. Abi Talib.

Thus, Umar b. al-Khattab came out of the Prophet's mosque and into the streets shouting and negating the news that the Prophet had died and even threatened to dismember anyone who said otherwise! Umar cried out, "Verily, the Messenger of Allah - by Allah - has not died, and will never die."[10] Although the Holy Prophet's body lay in wait, Umar continued to say that his soul had gone to Heaven like the soul of Prophet Isa[11] and promised a resurrection by saying, "The Prophet will come back."[12]

---

[8] *Tarikh al-Tabari*, 3:198; Ibn al-Atheer, 5:157

[9] *Al-Uqdul Farid*, 3:63

[10] *Tarikh al-Tabari*, 2:442; *Sirat Ibn Hisham*, 4:305

[11] Al-Shahrestani, *Al-Milal wal-Nihal*, Vol. 115; *Sunan al-Darimi*, Vol. 1

[12] Ibn Katheer, *Al-Kamil fil Tarikh*, 2:323; *Sirat Ibn Hisham*, 4:305

Upon Abu Bakr's return, Umar informed him about the undisclosed meeting at Saqifah and both of them headed out, along with Abu Ubaydah b. al-Jarrah, to the meeting.

The Saqifah meeting played out like a well-rehearsed theatrical production. Having been given some details about the meeting, Umar and Abu Bakr entered and found the Ansar locked in a bitter dispute. Sensing that the leadership was about to fall into the hands of Sa'd b. Ibadah from the Tribe of Khazraj, Abu Bakr immediately began to play on the emotions of the Tribe of Aws to provoke them so that they would not pay allegiance to their opponent, however his ultimate intention was to put forward his own proposal.

After sympathizing with the Aws, Abu Bakr then turned the tables and said that they (the Quraysh) were better suited for leadership than any other group. Abu Bakr said, "We, the Muhajireen were the first to accept Islam; we possess the most notable pedigree; our abode is the most central; we have the best leaders; and we are nearest of kin to the Prophet of Allah." Abu Bakr then appeased both tribes by saying that they too were worthy for some form of leadership of the ummah but that ultimate authority must reside with the Muhajireen. Abu Bakr continued his argument by quoting the words of the Prophet, "My successors are twelve...," but instead of saying, "...and all of them are from Bani Hashim,"[13] he changed it and said, "...and all of them are from Quraysh."[14] To which Umar seconded his statement.

However, a member of the Ansar, al-Habbab b. al-Mandhar, saw through Abu Bakr's facade. He realized the ploy being undertaken and quickly discredited their claim to leadership. Al-Habbab claimed that since the Ansar were the ones who approached the Prophet and supported him throughout his entire mission, that they had the first right for leadership. After his statement, the tone of the meeting rapidly intensified as fiery words were exchanged between him and Umar b. al-

---

[13] Al-Qanduzi, *Yanabi al-Muwaddah*, c. 77

[14] Abu Nuaym, *Haliyat al-Awliyaa*, 1:86

Khattab, which eventually led to Umar physically assaulting him and breaking his nose.

Abu Bakr immediately pacified the firestorm and proposed two candidates from the Quraysh for the position of caliph, Abu Ubaydah b. al-Jarrah and Umar b. al-Khattab. Abu Bakr declared, "I advise you to choose one of those two men, so pay allegiance to whomsoever you like."

By offering the caliphate to others, Abu Bakr absolved himself of any accusations that he might be seeking the caliphate for himself. However, Abu Ubaydah b. al-Jarrah immediately declined the offer, and Umar b. al-Khattab promptly interrupted Abu Bakr by taking up the Arab custom of respecting the elderly and stated, "God forbid that we do that, while you are alive amongst us," to Abu Bakr.

Then Umar, as if on cue, abruptly held out his hand towards Abu Bakr and said, "Stretch out your hand, and I will pay allegiance to you." Some of the Ansar agreed, namely: Ma'adh b. Jabal, Usayd b. Hudayr, Basheer b. Sa'd, and Zayd b. Thabit. They stood up and declared (on the grounds that the Prophet was from the Muhajireen, hence his successor should also be from the Muhajireen), "As we supported the Prophet, we will support his successor."[15]

Upon seeing the members of the Ansar offer allegiance to Abu Bakr, Umar related, "My heart was strengthened and others followed them."[16] Hence, that ended the nomination process by confirming Abu Bakr as the *khalifah* of the ummah.[17] Abu Bakr accepted gracefully saying, "May Allah reward you with goodness, O people of the Ansar."[18] Afterwards, in his own words, Umar b. al-Khattab stated, "The Quraysh examined [the situation] and chose a leader for themselves, and they were successful in their choice."[19]

---

[15] *Sirat Ibn Hisham*, 4:494

[16] *Al-Kamil fil al-Tarikh*, 2:231

[17] *Musnad Ahmad*, 1:239, 405, & 442; *Tarikh al-Madinah al-Munawarah*, 3:1006

[18] *Musnad Ahmad*, 5:185

[19] *Tarikh al-Tabari*, 5:13; Ibn al-Atheer, *Al-Kamil fil al-Tarikh*, 3:63 & 3:288

However, it can be seen that the caliphate was predetermined and confined to three people: Abu Bakr, Umar b. al-Khattab, and Abu Ubaydah b. al-Jarrah - hence, their conversation was not spontaneous.

As mentioned earlier, the members of the Quraysh, in particular: Abu Bakr, Umar b. al-Khattab, Abu Ubaydah b. al-Jarrah, al-Mugheerah b. Shu'bah, Abd al-Rahman b. Auf, Khalid b. al-Waleed, Muhammad b. Muslim, Ma'adh b. Jabal, Basheer b. Sa'd, and Usayd b. Hudayr had already agreed to this sequence of events long before the Saqifah meeting occurred, just like they had agreed that Abu Bakr would take control on behalf of the Tribe of Taym first.

Most of the others present followed Umar in giving their allegiance to Abu Bakr,[20] but the core of the Ansar who supported Ali b. Abi Talib refused, maintaining, "We will not pay allegiance to anyone except Ali b. Abi Talib."[21] The only leader of the Ansar who remained steadfast and refused to pay allegiance to Abu Bakr was Sa'd b. Ibadah, who was ill and unable to move. He told Umar, "By Allah, if I was able to stand, you would have heard from me a roaring which would have filled the streets and alleyways of Madinah and would have been painful to you and your companions."[22] He then turned to Abu Bakr and said, "I will never pay allegiance to you! Even if Ali pays allegiance, I still will not do so." In return, despite his illness, Umar assaulted him just as he had accosted al-Habbab b. al-Mandhar.[23]

Later on Umar recounted, "We attacked Sa'd b. Ibadah, and he was then trampled and the people said, 'Sa'd has been killed.'" Therefore, Umar said, "May Allah kill Sa'd." Perceiving him as a threat, Umar accused Sa'd b. Ibadah of hypocrisy and wanting the leadership for himself and hence wanted to kill him, but Abu Bakr restrained him.[24]

---

[20] *Al-Imamah wal-Siyasah*, Vol. 9

[21] *Tarikh al-Tabari*, 2:446 & 3:198; *Sahih al-Bukhari*, 4:111; *Musnad Ahmad b. Hanbal*, 1:55

[22] *Tarikh al-Tabari*, 2:459

[23] *Tarikh al-Tabari*, 2:457-463

[24] *Tarikh al-Tabari*, 2:459

If Sa'd b. Ibadah had really sought leadership, he could have obtained it easily since the Saqifah (shaded area) was his home territory and he was favored among the Muslims. Most likely, he would have obtained the caliphate much easier than Abu Bakr, but like Ali b. Abi Talib later said, Sa'd b. Ibadah was upset when he saw the people giving allegiance to Abu Bakr, not because he wanted the leadership for himself, but because he wanted the leadership to go to Ali, as the Prophet had dictated. Thereafter, Sa'd b. Ibadah rode to Huran in Syria, where after the death of Abu Bakr, Umar determined his fate by sending Muhammad b. Muslim to kill him.[25 & 26]

The events of Saqifah did not end on that day. Umar's primary concern was not to channel the political leadership towards Abu Bakr, but rather to keep it away from Ali b. Abi Talib. Umar sought to prevent Ali and the Bani Hashim from reaching the *khalifah* by any means possible. Thus after he became *khalifah*, Umar ensured that Uthman would succeed him, despite knowing that he would bring his tribesmen from the Bani Umayyah to power. Umar later said to Uthman, "Uthman, what keeps me from appointing you is your bigotry (*asabiyah*), and the preference that you give to your family and clan over other Muslims."[27] Still, Umar handed the rein of *khalifah* to Uthman, who as Umar had predicted, ruled by nepotism and favoritism until a defiant faction of the Muslims murdered him.

Overall, as Ibn Abil Hadid says,[28] "It was Umar who stood strongly behind Abu Bakr and paved the way for him to assume the leadership. If

---

[25] *Ansab al-Ashraf*, 1:589; Abd al-Fattah Abd al-Maqsud, *Al-Saqifah wal-Khalifah*, 13; *Al-Aqd al-Farid*, 4:247

[26] For further reference regarding the death of Sa'd b. Ibadah see, *Al-Khulafa al-Rashidun* by the Egyptian author Taha Husain, p.33. He says in his book that politics killed Sa'd b. Ibadah, meaning that they wanted to keep him away from power because they deemed his as a threat to the regime, and he was a man who insisted that the *khalifah* and the succession goes to the rightful people, the people appointed by Allah.

[27] *Tarikh al-Tabari*, 3:292

[28] Ibn Abil Hadid, *Sharh Nahjul-Balaghah*, 1:174

he had not backed him, it would have been impossible for Abu Bakr to reach where he reached [the *khalifah*]." Nonetheless, the fate of the ummah was sealed on that day, a day which Umar b. al-Khattab himself later called, "One of the errors of pre-Islamic times (*Faltah*[29] *min falataat al-jahiliyyah*)."[30] Even more he said, "Whoever goes back to it [the same method used to select Abu Bakr as the *khalifah*], then kill him."[31] Umar also admitted his mistake by saying, "God protected the Muslims from the dangers and risks of this immense error [meaning having elected Abu Bakr]."[32]

Nonetheless, the effects of Saqifah are felt even today. Had the Saqifah not happened and had the Muslims followed the Prophet's command, then most likely, there would be no Sunni or Shia Muslim. The Muslims would have been united under the banner of obedience to Allah and the leadership that Allah Himself ordained. Instead, once others obtained power, they held it firmly and did not allow anyone else outside their circle to share in it. As a result, they held absolute control over the ummah until the fall of the Bani Umayyah.

It can be argued that the issue of political leadership is solely a political issue and something to be left, buried in the past. Nevertheless, the influence of the ruling group extended beyond politics because for nearly 100 years they banned the transcription of the Prophet's sayings for fear that the narrations referring to the right and merits of Ali b. Abi Talib to the caliphate spread among the masses. As a result of not recording the hadith until centuries later, scholars had to argue over which statements of the Holy Prophet were authentic and which were fabrications and this led to the need to develop the Science of Hadith.

---

[29] In this context, the term *"faltah"* can be defined with any of the following: an unexpected event, a sudden occurrence, a slip or lapse, and something that only happens once and would never happen again.

[30] *Tarikh al-Tabari*, 2:459

[31] Ibn Abil Hadid, *Sharh Nahjul-Balaghah*, 2:29

[32] Ibid

Perhaps the most damaging of all was that the ummah was deprived from a valuable source of Divinely inspired guidance.

Given the severe calamity that the shift in leadership brought, one might ask: Why did Ali b. Abi Talib not fight for his right to lead the ummah? The answer is best given in his own words:

> O Allah! I beseech Thee to take revenge on the Quraysh and those who are assisting them, for they have cut asunder my kinship and overturned my cup and have collaborated to contest a right to which I was entitled more than anyone else. They said to me, 'If you get your right, that will be just, but if you are denied the right that too will be just. Endure it with sadness or kill yourself in grief.' I looked around but found no one to shield me, protect me, or help me except the members of my family. I refrained from flinging them into death and therefore closed my eyes despite the dust; kept swallowing saliva despite the suffocation of grief; and endured pangs of anger although it was bitterer than colocynth and more grievous than the bite of knives.[33]

Although Ali b. Abi Talib knew that the ummah would suffer without his leadership, he also knew that it would destroy itself if he attempted to take the leadership by force; and thus he abstained from the caliphate until the murder of Uthman. Even then, he was still hesitant, but at that moment in time, Islam was on the brink of annihilation and there was no one else to save it except for him. However, the extent of the damage done by the group, unfortunately, had already severely crippled the Muslim ummah.

---

[33] *Nahjul Balaghah*, Sermon 217

Chapter 4
Political Policies of Quraysh

﴿وَالَّذِينَ اسْتَجَابُوا لِرَبِّهِمْ وَأَقَامُوا الصَّلَاةَ وَأَمْرُهُمْ
شُورَىٰ بَيْنَهُمْ وَمِمَّا رَزَقْنَاهُمْ يُنفِقُونَ﴾

*Those who hearken to their Lord, and establish regular prayer;
who (conduct) their affairs by mutual consultation; who spend out
of what We bestow on them for sustenance.*

Holy Qur'an, 42:38

Political Practices of the Quraysh Group

After securing the caliphate, the Quraysh group turned its attention to
seizing authority of the various regions. Thus, whoever posed a threat or
was uncooperative with the new powers was quickly removed from
their positions. This meant the removal of competent and experienced
people, including members of their own families, such as the removal of
Umar b. al-Khattab's two sons, Zayd b. al-Khattab and Ubaydallah b. al-
Khattab, as well as the removal of Abu Bakr's son, Abdul Rahman b. Abu
Bakr.

In their place, Umar appointed more conforming men, such as Sa'd b.
Abi al-Waqqas to govern Kufa, Abu Musa al-Ashari to govern Basra, and
Mu'awiyah b. Abu Sufyan to govern Shaam (Syria). By including non-
Quraysh members into the administration, the party reflected an
illusionary bi-partisan government.

Before assuming the role of the third caliph, Uthman b. al-Affan had
agreed to follow all of the policies of his predecessors, Abu Bakr and

Umar b. al-Khattab; however, after becoming caliph, he reverted to the pre-Islamic Arab custom of nepotism.

Fully aware of Uthman's tendencies to backslide and knowing that the masses despised favoritism, Umar warned him that the Quraysh would lose their power if he did not refrain from nepotism,[1] however Uthman did not heed his warning. Unlike Abu Bakr and Umar, Uthman filled the official positions with his own tribesmen - people who were undeniably incompetent individuals, such as Abu Sufyan, Marwan b. al-Hakam, Mu'awiyah b. Abu Sufyan, Al-Waleed b. Uqbah, Abdullah b. Abi Sarh, and Sa'ed b. al-Aas.

In doing so, he incensed many companions of the Prophet - even those who had previously sided with the Quraysh such as Lady Aishah, the wife of the Prophet. Particularly upset were those who lost power - not because of their incompetence, but rather, due to Uthman's nepotism - people such as Amr b. al-Aas, who lost Egypt; al-Mugheerah b. Shu'bah, who lost Kufa; and Abu Musa al-Ashari, who lost Basra. To replace them, Uthman appointed other inept and corrupt individuals from the Bani Umayyah. As a result, some of those townships revolted, and in Kufa for example, the people ousted Uthman's choice and reinstated Abu Musa al-Ashari.[2] It appears that Uthman was not interested in restoring order and credibility to the government, but rather, to fill the offices with his own family members, even though they had no qualification, experience, or integrity.

Uthman's nepotism eventually led to his assassination and the awaited succession of Ali b. Abi Talib to the caliphate in 35 AH. After the Khawarij murdered Ali b. Abi Talib during his caliphate, the power base once again shifted to the Quraysh group under the rule of Mu'awiyah b. Abu Sufyan.

Learning from Uthman's errors, Mu'awiyah balanced political office by incorporating tribal groups and making use of Umar's practice of

---

[1] Ibn al-Atheer, *Al-Kamil fil-Tarikh*, 3:67

[2] Ibn Sa'd, *Al-Tabaqat*, 5:33

appointing allies from outside his tribe to official positions. Hence, Amr b. al-Aas, al-Mugheerah b. al-Shu'bah, Abu Huraira, al-Numan b. Basheer, and Abdul Rahman b. Khalid all found places in the new administration of Mu'awiyah. He went as far as learning how to appease Lady Aishah, a woman who was known to voice her opposition against those whom she deemed as a roadblock in the way of her own objectives, such as Ali b. Abi Talib and Uthman b. al-Affan.

Selection of the First Six Caliphs

Somewhere along the line of Muslim history, a misconception arose that the caliphate was first instituted by *shura* (free and popular election). Although, this misconception concurs very well with contemporary democratic theories and promotes Islam as being a conventional and democratic religion, the truth of the matter is that the office of "caliphate" was not brought into being by a popular vote, nor was it supposed to be. The office of the caliph, like the governance of prophethood, is not one to be determined by consultation, but rather by Divine ordination.

In Islam, governance encompasses all facets of life - social, religious, political, economical, judicial, etc. and thus, it is based on Allah's laws and instructions. Hence, the notion that a democratic process (an assembly of men "chosen" by the people) occurred in the appointment of Abu Bakr's leadership is not accurate.

As mentioned earlier, the first caliph was decided by two people: Umar b. al-Khattab and Abu Ubayd b. al-Jarrah who both declined their bid for election and instead nominated Abu Bakr and coaxed the others to follow suit at Saqifah.

After Saqifah, Ali b. Abi Talib said to Umar b. al-Khattab, "Today you are consolidating and supporting Abu Bakr so that tomorrow he will support you and bring you as his successor."[3] His words rang true since two and a half years later, Umar reaped the benefits of his stance when

---

[3] Ibn Qutaybah, *Al-Imamah wal-Siyasah*, 1:11

Abu Bakr appointed him as his successor before his death. Their pact did not escape going unnoticed by others because even Mu'awiyah b. Abu Sufyan concluded, "They agreed upon that and there was harmony between them."[4]

The selection of the third caliph, Uthman b. al-Affan also tends to be a subject of some misconception. As the death of the second caliph Umar neared, he called on a council of six people to determine the next leader. On the surface, this may seem like a semi-electoral body; however, Umar instructed his son Abdullah, "If they appoint Uthman as their leader, they will get the most out of it."[5]

Earlier, when Hudayfah, a scribe of the Qur'an asked Umar b. al-Khattab who would succeed him, Umar said, "Uthman b. al-Affan."[6] As in the previous accord of Abu Bakr and Umar, Uthman b. al-Affan allied with his cousin, Abdul Rahman b. Auf to mutually support each other for the position of the caliphate during the six council "election" meeting.

As Ali b. Abi Talib narrates, "There was a council of six, and the Muslims were supposed to choose one out of those six, but Abdul Rahman b. Auf favored Uthman, so that tomorrow Uthman would favor him and make him his successor."[7]

After the appointment of Uthman, and later into his office, Abdul Rahman incited the people to revolt against Uthman, and thus Uthman excluded him from ever being appointed as caliph, which severed their relationship to the point where they never spoke to one another throughout the remainder of their lives.[8]

Due to the subtleties of this arrangement, the appointment of Uthman to the caliphate continues until today to be seen as a form of

---

[4] Al-Mas'udi, *Muruj al-Dhahabi*, 3:12

[5] Ibn Shabah, *Tarikh al-Madinah al-Munawarah*, 2:148

[6] Al-Muttaqi al-Hindi, *Kanz al-Umal*, 5:727, hadith 14259

[7] Ibn al-Atheer, *Al-Kamil fil-Tarikh*, 3:71

[8] *Tarikh al-Tabari*, 3:294

election by some. History is clear that when Mu'awiyah b. Abu Sufyan came into power, he reserved the caliphate exclusively for his own son and began the first dynasty in the history of Islam.

What history reports less of is that he also maintained the same political ties as the Quraysh group who had diverted the flow of political power to their advantage. To that end, he made pacts with Amr b. al-Aas, Talha b. Ubaydillah,[9] Zubayr b. al-Awam,[10] and Abu Musa al-Ashari, all of whom disfavored Ali, by offering them governorships in exchange for service.

When he asked Amr b. al-Aas to fight against Ali b. Abi Talib for him, Amr b. al-Aas replied, "I will not sell my faith to you unless you give me something in this world here." Hence, Mu'awiyah appointed him as the governor of Egypt.[11] Similarly, Mu'awiyah enlisted Talha and Zubayr in the fight against Imam Ali in return for rule over some of the other states.[12] Mu'awiyah also promised Abu Musa al-Ashari, "If you pay allegiance to me and support my position, I will utilize your two sons; one of them will be the governor of Kufa, and the other will be the governor of Basra."[13] In this way, Mu'awiyah continued the work that his predecessors had begun in channeling the political authority and wealth of the Muslims into a pre-determined and selected group of hands.

Although the caliphate was the main prize, the Quraysh group did not limit their efforts to it. After installing Abu Bakr as the first caliph, they slowly began acquiring governorships of the outlying provinces. As

---

[9] Talha b. Ubaydillah was one of the companions who was known for his strong opposition against Uthman. He was killed by his friend Marwan b. Hakim in the Battle of Camel, 36 AH and is buried outside Basra.

[10] Zubayr b. Awam was born twenty-eight years before the Hijrah. He embraced Islam at the age of fifteen. He was the son of Saffiah b. Abdul Muttalib, the aunt of the Prophet. He married Asmah b. Abu Bakr. He was killed in 36 AH in the Battle of Camel, which was spearheaded by Aishah against Imam Ali. He is buried near Basra, Iraq.

[11] *Waqat Siffeen*, p. 34-39; *Tarikh b. Khaldun*, 2:625

[12] Ibid

[13] Al-Dhahabi, *Sirr Alam al-Nubala*, 2:396

is the case in the modus operandi of the Quraysh, they appointed their political allies to the governorships. The main objective of their appointments was to enlist individuals that did not oppose them and any inclination of strife towards their leadership would be met with expulsion, even at the expense of their own relatives.

As noted earlier, Umar b. al-Khattab's two sons, Zayd b. al-Khattab and Ubaydallah b. al-Khattab were both ostracized, as was Abdul Rahman b. Abu Bakr, the son of Abu Bakr. Instead, Umar appointed Sa'd b. Abi al-Waqqas to govern Kufa, Abu Musa al-Ashari to govern Basra, and Mu'awiyah b. Abu Sufyan to govern Syria. Their true intention was to maintain control of the rapidly expanding Muslim empire among themselves. The issue was not one of election or selection; it was one of maintaining political hegemony within a select group of people.

Harmony or otherwise, the important fact to note is that Umar was appointed by Abu Bakr, not elected to the caliphate, unlike the case with Abu Bakr.

Despite the sheer number of hadith in both Sunni and Shia sources, which declared Ali b. Abi Talib to be the rightful political successor to the Prophet, still many opponents of the Ahlul Bayt in modern times object to the concept of an appointed successor on the basis that it is nepotistic and undemocratic. If so, then how do they explain and accept the fact that none of the first three caliphs arrived at the caliphate through a "democratic" election?

Muslim history has noted that the Saqifah meeting in itself turned into an ad-hoc assembly, and that the explicit appointment of the three caliphs was a premeditated maneuver by a group to bypass the leadership of Ali. Yet still, they argued against the Prophet appointing Ali. Furthermore, if nepotism is cited (because Ali was a relative of the Prophet) then the same argument can be posed when Uthman's relatives, such as Mu'awiyah, Yazid, and others were chosen as caliphs. Hence, it would be unfounded to claim that the caliphate was first instituted by *shura* (consultation).

Dialogue between Abdullah b. al-Abbas and Umar b. al-Khattab

Abdullah b. al-Abbas (who is from the tribe of Bani Hashim and was the first cousin of Ali and the Prophet) and Umar b. al-Khattab held many discussions. On one occasion, during the caliphate of Umar they debated whether the Bani Hashim should hold the caliphate. This dialogue is of particular interest, since it highlights the issues at hand.[14]

Umar, "Do you know why the people did not elect you [the family of the Prophet] to the caliphate?"

Ibn Abbas, "No, I do not know."

Umar, "I know what the reason was."

Ibn Abbas, "What was it?"

Umar, "The Quraysh hated to see the prophethood and caliphate vested in one house. If that would have happened, you would have wronged the people!"

Ibn Abbas, "Can Amir al-Mumineen (Umar) control his anger if I want to say something?"

Umar, "Feel free to say whatever you want to say."

Ibn Abbas, "If you say that Quraysh hated to see this [prophethood and caliphate vested in one family] then (know that) in the Qur'an, Allah has said about some of the companions [who had lived during the time of the Prophet], "That is because they hate the revelation of Allah, so He has made their deeds fruitless."[15] And if you say that we [Bani Hashim] will do injustice if both the prophethood and caliphate are vested in our family, then if we are supposed to do mischief, we will do mischief even without being caliphs or successors, simply because we are the family of the Prophet and the closest people to him. However, we will not do that because our stance, morality, and attitude mirror the attitude of the

---

[14] *Tarikh al-Tabari*, 5:30; *Qasas al-Arab*, 2:363; Ibn al-Atheer, *Al-Kamil fil-Tarikh*, 3:63; Ibn Abil Hadid, *Sharh Nahjul-Balaghah*, 3:107

[15] *Holy Qur'an*, 47:9

Prophet, about whom Allah says, "Verily, you stand on an exalted standard of character."[16] Also Allah said, "Lower your wing to the believers who follow you."[17] We will not depart from him (the Prophet), so why are you worried that if we become caliphs we will do mischief? If you say, "The Quraysh chose Abu Bakr and Umar," then Allah answers, "Your Lord creates and chooses as He pleases. No choices have they in the matter."[18] Plus you know Umar, that Allah has chosen certain people from among His creatures to lead humanity. If the Quraysh had joined their vision with the plan of Allah, then the community would have been prosperous and successful."

Umar, "Calm down Ibn Abbas. You members of the Bani Hashim, your heart only wanted to deceive the Quraysh permanently, and you hold perpetual hatred and animosity towards the Quraysh."

Ibn Abbas, "Calm down Umar, do not say that the hearts of Bani Hashim are deceitful. Their hearts are part of the heart of the Messenger of Allah. It is the same heart of the Messenger of Allah that Allah has cleansed and purified, and they are the family of the Prophet whom Allah describes as, "Allah only wishes to remove all abomination from you, O members of the family of the Prophet, and to make you pure and immaculate."[19] If you speak about animosity and grudges in our hearts, this would be natural given that our right has been usurped from us and it is in the hands of a transgressor."

Umar, "What are you saying Ibn Abbas? I have heard some bad things about you, and if I mention them to you, I would lose respect for you in my eyes."

Ibn Abbas, "What have you heard about me? Tell me. If it is false, I will defend myself. If it is true, I will never lose respect for you in my eyes."

---

[16] *Holy Qur'an*, 68:4

[17] *Holy Qur'an*, 26:215

[18] *Holy Qur'an*, 28:68

[19] *Holy Qur'an*, 33:33

Umar, "I have heard you telling people that this issue [the *khalifah*] was taken from the family of the Prophet out of jealousy and by way of injustice."

Ibn Abbas, "Regarding jealousy, yes it is true because *Iblis* (Satan) was jealous of Adam and forced him out of Paradise. We are the children of Adam, and there is always jealousy among us. If you say "transgression," you know better who has the right in this matter [the *khalifah*], and you Umar are the best person to answer this question. Did you not say that the Arabs are closer to the non-Arabs to the Prophet, and did you not say that the Quraysh are closer than the other tribes are to the Prophet? If you have said that and if you come to the Quraysh, then who among them is closest to the Prophet? Of course, they are the Bani Hashim. I am using the same analogy that you used. We have more right to the caliphate than anyone from the Quraysh."

Umar, "Stand up and go home."

Ibn Abbas stood up and as he was leaving Umar said, "You who are leaving, come back! Despite what has happened between us, you are still respected in my eyes."

Ibn Abbas answered, "You who are the caliph now, we also have to preserve your right."

After Ibn Abbas left, Umar turned to the people around him and said, "I never saw Ibn Abbas discuss something with anyone and not defeat him."

Chapter 5
Backlash

﴿إِنَّمَا يُرِيدُ ٱللَّهُ لِيُذْهِبَ عَنكُمُ ٱلرِّجْسَ أَهْلَ ٱلْبَيْتِ وَيُطَهِّرَكُمْ تَطْهِيـراً﴾

Allah only wishes to remove all abomination from you, O members of the Family, and to make you pure and immaculate.

Holy Qur'an, 33:33

Attempt to Burn the House of Fatima al-Zahra

The day after the Saqifah, Umar b. al-Khattab, along with a group of individuals came to the house of the daughter of the Holy Prophet. In the house, there was Ali b. Abi Talib, Fatima, and their two sons, Hasan and Husayn, who were still in a state of deep sorrow over the death of the Prophet.

Fatima opened the door and asked Umar, "Did you come here to burn our house?" Umar retorted, "Yes, unless you enter into what the nation entered in [meaning allegiance to Abu Bakr]."[1] Umar then slammed open the door against Fatima at which point she found herself being squeezed between the door and the wall of her house, causing one of her ribs to break. At that time, she was pregnant with the third grandson of the Holy Prophet; however, the force that Umar applied on the door caused her to have a miscarriage, and the baby who had been named Muhsin by the Prophet, was stillborn only a few days after the death of his grandfather.

---

[1] *Tarikh al-Tabari*, 3:198; *Tarikh Abul Fida*, 1:156

Many historians have narrated this event with some of them providing details that others omit. Ibn Abd Rabah al-Andalusi says:[2]

> Those who refrained from giving the *bayah* (allegiance) to Abu Bakr were Ali, Abbas (the uncle of the Prophet), Zubayr b. al-Awam (cousin of the Prophet) and Sa'd b. Ibadah. As for Ali and Abbas, they sat in the house of Fatima until Abu Bakr sent Umar to take them out of the house of Fatima, and he (Abu Bakr) said to him (Umar), "If they refuse, then fight them." Thus, he (Umar) came with a torch of fire to engulf the house on them and upon arriving, he encountered Fatima. She said, "O Ibn al-Khattab, did you come to burn our house?" He said, "Yes, unless you enter into what the ummah entered into."

Al-Tabari also relates the story; however, he says that Talha, Zubayr, and some men from the Muhajireen were also in the house. He goes on to say that Umar told them, "By Allah, I will burn the house unless you come out for the *bayah* (allegiance)." Raising his sword, Zubayr came out of the house, but he fell to the ground and was attacked. In the ensuing chaos, his sword was taken away.[3]

Ibn Abil Hadid says:

> When Fatima saw what Umar did, she cried and wailed, and many women from Bani Hashim gathered with her. They came to her and she said, "O Abu Bakr, how fast you launched your strike on the family of the Prophet after the death of the Prophet. By Allah, I will never speak to you until I meet Allah!"[4]

The historian, al-Baladri reports:

---

[2] Ibn Abd Rabbah al-Andalusi, *Al-Aqd al-Farid*, 4:259

[3] *Tarikh al-Tabari*, 2:198

[4] Ibn Abil Hadid, *Sharh Nahjul-Balaghah*, 2.:119

> Abu Bakr sent for Ali, asking him to pay allegiance. He didn't pay allegiance and thus Umar came with a torch to the house of Ali and Fatima. He came face to face with Fatima and she said to him, "Are you really going to burn the door of the house?" Umar answered, "Yes indeed."[5]

Other Sunni authors go on to state that had Fatima al-Zahra not opened the door, Umar would have proceeded to burn down the entire house. They say that Umar was shouting from outside the house saying, "Burn the house with the people inside it!"[6] The companions who were around Umar saw him gathering wood and warned him, "Umar, you know that Fatima lives in this house." Umar answered, "Still, even if she lives here I am going to burn the house!"[7]

Some other narrations have unsubstantially claimed that an opposition group had gathered at the house of Fatima ready to act against Abu Bakr. However, the truth is that some of the previously mentioned prominent Sunni historians do not mention this at all – scholars such as al-Shahristani, al-Baladri, al-Safti, al-Jawhari, Ibn Abd Rabbah al-Andalusi, and Urwat b. Zubayr. Thus, this claim was just an excuse put forth later on in order to justify the actions of Umar and his group.

These prominent Sunni scholars also name the individuals who participated with Umar in the attack on Fatima al-Zahra's home and they include the following: Ubayd b. Hubayr, Thabit b. Qays, Muhammad b. Muslim, Khalid b. al-Waleed, al-Mugheerah b. Shu'bah, Abu Ubaydah b. al-Jarrah, Sa'd Mawla Abi Udaybah, Ma'adh b. Jabal, Qunfud, Uthman, Abd al-Rahman b. Auf, Ziyad b. Ubayd, Mu'awiyah b. Abu Sufyan, and Amr b. al-Aas.

---

[5] Al-Baladri, *Ansab al-Ashraf*, 1:586

[6] Shahrestani, *Al-Milal wal-Nihal*, 1:56; Salah al-Din al-Susti; Al-Shafi'i, *Manaqib al-Ibadah*, 3:407

[7] Ibn Qutaybah, *Al-Imamah wal-Siyasah*, 1:12; Umar Ridha (Kahhalah), *Alam Al-Nisa*, 4:14; Abd al-Fattah Abd al-Maqsud; *Al-Saqifah wal-Khalifah*, 14

Many years later at a meeting between Imam Hasan (the first grandson of the Prophet and son of Fatima and Ali) and Mu'awiyah b. Abu Sufyan in the presence of Mugheerah b. Shu'bah, the Imam said to Mugheerah, "You are the one who hit Fatima,[8] the daughter of the Prophet until you made her bleed and she miscarried her baby. You wanted to humiliate the Prophet, and you opposed his teachings and violated the respect of the Prophet. You know that the Prophet said to Fatima al-Zahra, 'You are the leader of the women of Paradise.' By Allah, your fate will be the Fire."[9]

Other Sunni historians who narrate this meeting are Ibn Qutaybah,[10] Ibn Abil Hadid,[11] and al-Mahqari.[12] However, as for Fatima's unborn son (who was killed during the attack), Ibn Qutaybah says that Muhsin b. Ali perished when he was a baby, but he does not mention how.[13]

Setting aside the events that occurred at the door of Fatima's home, did Umar have the right to enter her home? According to the Holy Qur'an, no one may enter another person's house without permission, as Allah orders:

﴿يَاأَيُّهَا ٱلَّذِينَ آمَنُواْ لاَ تَدْخُلُواْ بُيُوتاً غَيْرَ بُيُوتِكُمْ حَتَّى تَسْتَأْنِسُواْ وَتُسَلِّمُواْ عَلَىٰ أَهْلِهَا ذَلِكُمْ خَيْرٌ لَّكُمْ لَعَلَّكُمْ تَذَكَّرُونَ. فَإِن لَّمْ تَجِدُوا فِيهَآ أَحَداً فَلاَ تَدْخُلُوهَا حَتَّى يُؤْذَنَ لَكُمْ وَإِن قِيلَ لَكُمُ ٱرْجِعُواْ فَٱرْجِعُواْ هُوَ أَزْكَى لَكُمْ وَٱللَّهُ بِمَا تَعْمَلُونَ عَلِيمٌ﴾

---

[8] When Umar attacked Fatima in her home, others physically accosted her as well.

[9] Al-Tabrasi, *Al-Ihtijaj*, 1:414

[10] Ibn Qutaybah, *Al-Imamah wal-Siyasah*, 1:12-13

[11] Ibn Abil Hadid, *Sharh Nahjul-Balaghah*, 14:192

[12] Al-Mahqari, *Waqt Siffeen*, 1:63

[13] Ibn Qutaybah, *Al-Ma'arif*, 1:93

O you who believe! Enter not the houses other than your [own] houses until you have sought familiarity and saluted their inhabitants; this is best for you; haply you may remember. But if you do not find anyone in there, then enter them not until permission is given to you; and if it is said unto you 'Go you back' then go back, for it is purer for you; and God knows what all of you do. (c. 24:27-28)

Even the Messenger of Allah did not enter the house of his daughter and grandchildren without first asking permission!

It is indeed disheartening that such an event occurred despite Allah's commandment that the ummah is to treat the family of the Prophet with adoration:

$$﴿قُل لاَّ أَسْأَلُكُمْ عَلَيْهِ أَجْراً إِلاَّ ٱلْمَوَدَّةَ فِى ٱلْقُرْبَى﴾$$

Say: 'I demand not of you any recompense for it (the toils of the apostleship) save the love of (my) relatives.' (c. 42:23)

Regret for the Actions Taken Against Fatima

As time passed, Abu Bakr felt the pangs of remorse about the incident at Fatima al-Zahra's home and said, "Every man sleeps next to his wife, embracing her, enjoying his family, and you left me with my misery. I don't need your *bayah*, I don't need it, take it away from me." Near the end of his life he also mentioned, "I was sad for three things that I did, and I wish I hadn't done them. One of them is that I exposed the house of Fatima."[14]

---

[14] *Lisan al Mizan*, 8:189; Ibn Qutaybah, *Al-Imamah wa Siyasah*, 1:18; Ibn Abil Hadid, *Sharh Nahjul-Balaghah*, 6:51; *Tarikh al-Ya'qubi*, 2:137

Perhaps Abu Bakr's guilt came from the fact that he had ordered Umar to subdue whoever was in the house if they did not surrender, even though he knew that those in the house included Fatima al-Zahra - the beloved daughter of the Holy Prophet and his grandsons, Hasan and Husayn. The guilt drove Abu Bakr to seek reconciliation, so he asked Umar to accompany him to reconcile with Fatima al-Zahra and said to Umar, "Since we have angered Fatima, let us go and make her happy."[15]

Initially, they sought permission from her to enter her house, but she refused, so they asked Ali and he allowed them in. Both Abu Bakr and Umar b. Khattab sat in front of Fatima al-Zahra, but she turned her head towards the wall.

Abu Bakr said to her, "O beloved daughter of the Prophet, you are dearer to me than my daughter Aishah, and I wish that on the day your father died, I would have died instead and that I would not have remained (alive) after him. You are angry because we did not grant you your inheritance since we heard your father say, 'We don't leave any inheritance; whatever we leave is charity.'"

With her head still turned against them, Fatima al-Zahra replied, "If I remind you of a saying of my father, would you acknowledge it, and if you acknowledge it, would you practice and implement it?" Both of them said they would and thus she said, "I ask you by Allah, did you not hear the Prophet of Allah saying, 'The pleasure of Fatima is my pleasure, and her wrath and anger is my anger, and whoever loves my daughter Fatima loves me, and whoever pleases her pleases me, and whoever angers her angers me?'"[16] They said, "Yes, we heard this from the Messenger of Allah." She continued, "Then I testify before Allah and His angels that you have angered me, and when I meet the Prophet, I will raise my grievances with you to him."

---

[15] Ibn Qutaybah, *Al-Imamah wal-Siyasah*, 1:14

[16] *Sahih al-Bukhari*, 5:36

According to al-Tabari,[17] al-Bukhari,[18] and al-Muslim,[19] Fatima al-Zahra refused to speak with Abu Bakr until she died. Even at her funeral, her wishes were for them not to be present, thus Ali buried her at night according to her wishes and did not allow Abu Bakr and Umar to participate in her burial.

The exact date when Fatima al-Zahra died is uncertain. According to Abul Faraj al-Isfahani,[20] she lived a maximum of six months after the death of her father, while others mention a minimum period of forty days. What the author upholds is that of the narration of Imam Muhammad al-Baqir, in which he stated she died three months after the departure of the Messenger of Allah.

Usurping the Land of Fadak

Muslim commentators report that when the verse, "And give your kin their rightful due" was revealed,[21] the Holy Prophet asked the Angel Gabriel what he was being directed to do, and Gabriel replied that Allah was commanding him to give Fadak, a piece of land north of Madinah, to his daughter Fatima al-Zahra and the Holy Prophet avidly complied.

However, after the death of the Prophet, Abu Bakr confiscated the land from Fatima on the pretext that the Holy Prophet had said, "We the prophets, do not leave any inheritance. Whatever we leave behind is charity." This is a statement that not only contradicts the wishes of the Prophet, but also a precedent of the Qur'an that states, "And Sulayman inherited from Dawud."[22]

Nevertheless, when Abu Bakr and Umar later came to power, they both gave preference to Lady Aishah. History narrates that on several

---

[17] *Tarikh al-Tabari*, 3:202

[18] *Sahih al-Bukhari*, 4:96

[19] *Sahih al-Muslim*, hadith 1259

[20] Abul Faraj al-Isfahani, *Maqatil al-Talibi'in*, 19

[21] *Holy Qur'an*, 17:26, 30:38

[22] *Holy Qur'an*, 27:16

occasions, the exception to their rule that "prophets do not leave inheritance" was enacted. For instance, both Abu Bakr and Umar allowed Lady Aishah to inherit the house of the Holy Prophet, although she did not have the absolute right to inherit the home exclusively, considering that she was merely one out of the nine wives of the Prophet, while the other wives were renounced of their share of the home inheritance. The property was hers and she exercised her control of it by permitting the burial of her father, Abu Bakr in the room of the Holy Prophet, next to the Prophet, while refusing the grandson of the Holy Prophet, Hasan to be buried next to his grandfather.

When Uthman came to power, Lady Aishah and Hafsah (two wives of the Prophet) asked him to grant them more of the inheritance of the Prophet, however Uthman rebuked Lady Aishah by saying, "Didn't you come here with another man named Malik b. Aus al-Nadhari and say that the Prophet said, 'We don't leave inheritance?' Didn't you prevent Fatima al-Zahra from taking her share of the inheritance of the Prophet, and now you have come to ask for your share?"

Enraged, Lady Aishah went to the Mosque of the Holy Prophet, raised the Prophet's shirt and cried that Uthman had disagreed with "the owner of this shirt." In turn, Uthman cited verse 66:10 of the Qur'an drawing a parallel about the disobedient wives of the prophets Nuh and Lut to her.

Ironically, Uthman did not return the land of Fadak to the children of Fatima al-Zahra nor allow Lady Aishah to have it, nor did he give it as charity, as the hadith that he was claiming to act under said. Instead, Uthman gave it as a gift to one of his family members named Marwan b. al-Hakam, whom the Holy Prophet had cursed and exiled from Madinah for his sedition and rampage against Islam.[23]

---

[23] Ibn Qutaybah, *Al-Marif*, 195; Ibn Abil Hadid, *Sharh Nahjul-Balaghah*

Story of Fadak

In the once populated Jewish territory of Khaybar, which is north of Madinah in a town known as Fadak, lay the start of one of the most contentious issues in the history of Islam - the right of inheritance of the Prophet's daughter, Fatima al-Zahra.

Both schools of thought (The School of the Ahlul Bayt - also known as the Shia; and The School of the Companions - also known as the Sunni) have their own version on how the episode regarding Fadak unfolded. The position of the School of the Companions is that the family of the Prophet had no right to inherit Fadak because the Prophet himself narrated that he does not leave behind any bequests; while the School of the Ahlul Bayt claim otherwise and add that Fadak was not only Fatima al-Zahra's right to inherit, but also that her father bestowed it to her during his lifetime by the decree of Allah. In addition, scholars who follow the Ahlul Bayt contest that by stripping Fatima of her resources also meant the weakening of Ali b. Abi Talib of the means to defend his rightful entitlement to the leadership of the community.

Both schools of thought relate that Fadak was a well-developed and productive farmland owned by the Jews of the Bani Nadir tribe (the Jews of Madinah) near Khaybar. The Jews who lived in Khaybar posed a persistent threat to the newly established Islamic community. Several attempts were made by them to destabilize and destroy the Islamic community, and thus the Prophet sent his army, led by Ali b. Abi Talib, to conquer their castle in the seventh year of the Hijrah. What remained after the acquisition was the Jewish village of Fadak.

After witnessing the defeat of Khaybar, the Jews of Fadak met with an envoy of the Prophet. Preferring survival, these Jews struck a settlement with the Prophet, and in this deal, they relinquished half of the settlement of Fadak. In addition, they also agreed to deliver half of their part of Fadak's yearly production to the Prophet, and in return, the Jewish villagers could live peacefully under the protection of the Islamic state.

Therefore, after conquering Khaybar and taking possession of half of the land of Fadak and its yearly revenues without embattlement, the attention then turned towards the issue of its ownership. In accordance with Islam, land or wealth acquired through military intervention becomes the property of the Muslim community; but in all other circumstances, land or wealth acquired without the use of military might becomes the sole property of the Prophet, as indicated in the Qur'an where Allah says:

﴿وَمَا أَفَاءَ اللّهُ عَلَى رَسُولِه مِنْهُمْ فَمَا أَوْجَفْتُمْ عَلَيْهِ مِنْ خَيْلٍ وَلَا رِكَابٍ وَلَكِنَّ اللّهَ يُسَلِّطُ رُسُلَهُ عَلَى مَن يَشَاءُ وَ اللّهُ عَلَى كُلِّ شَيْءٍ قَدِيرٌ﴾

What God has bestowed on His Apostle and taken away from them - for this you made no expedition with either cavalry or camels: but God gives power to His apostles over any He pleases: and God has power over all things. (c. 59:6)

Allah further adds in the following verse:

﴿مَا أَفَاءَ اللّهُ عَلَى رَسُولِه مِنْ أَهْلِ الْقُرَى فَلِلّهِ وَلِلرَّسُولِ وَلِذِي الْقُرْبَى ﴾

What God has bestowed on His Apostle and taken away from the people of the townships belongs to God, to His Apostle and to kindred and orphans... (c. 59:7)

Thus, the followers of the Ahlul Bayt have long claimed that Fadak belonged to the Prophet and their belief is based on the Qur'anic verses mentioned above (c. 59:6-7), in addition to the recorded traditions.

According to the School of the Companions, they too believe that Fadak was the property of the Prophet since it was acquired without the use of force.[24] For example, it is narrated in the Sunni books of tradition that Umar is reported to have said, "The property of Bani Nadir was among that which Allah bestowed on His Messenger; against them neither horses nor camels were pricked, but they belonged specifically to the Messenger of Allah."[25]

Therefore, the matter of Allah granting ownership of Fadak to the Prophet is not disputed in either school of thought. The disagreement amongst the schools began in regards to what the Prophet did with Fadak during his lifetime, and thus, they narrate the story of Fadak differently.

Shia scholars believe that during his lifetime, the Prophet bestowed Fadak upon his daughter Fatima al-Zahra. These scholars cite a letter written by Ali b. Abi Talib to the governor of Basra, Uthman b. Hunaif in which he stated, "Yes, Fadak was the only land under the heavens which was in our possession; but the inclinations of certain men lusted for it and the souls of others relinquished it."

On the other hand, those who deny that the Prophet presented Fadak to Fatima al-Zahra reason that the notion that the Prophet would grant one of his children such an abundant gift and would neglect the others is unimaginable. They reason that this would mean that the Prophet would have acted contrary to the Islamic concept of parental fairness, since he had more children other than Fatima. In order to defend this theory, they cite the following tradition, "The companion Basheer b. Sa'd came to the Prophet telling him that he had given one of his sons a garden as a gift and requested the Prophet to be a witness thereto. The

---

[24] Al-Tabari, *The Last Years of the Prophet* (English translation), 4:196; *Futuhal Buldan*, p.42; *Tarikh al-Khamees*, 2:64; Ibn Atheer, *Tarikh al-Kamil*, 2:85; Ibn Hisham, *Seerah*, 3:48; Ibn Khuldun, *Al-Tarikh*, 2, part 2

[25] *Sahih al-Bukhari*, 4:46, 7:82, & 9:121-22; *Sahih al-Muslim*, 5:151; Abu Dawood, *Sunan*, 3:139-41; Nasa'i, *Sunan*, 7:132; Ahmad al-Hanbal, al-*Musnad*, p.25, 48, 60, & 208; Al-Kubra (Al-Bayhaqi), *Sunan*, 6:296-99

Prophet asked whether he had given a similar gift to all of his children. When he replied that he had not done so, then the Prophet told him, 'Go away, for I will not be a witness to injustice.'"[26]

The Ahlul Bayt rebut that the Prophet acted fairly when he presented Fadak to Fatima al-Zahra for several reasons. Firstly, Fatima was no ordinary child from the Prophet's children; and he showed her a lofty position through his exceptional treatment towards her. For example, he would stand up to greet her, offer his seat to her, and only permit the door to her home to be adjacent to his home and the mosque. The Prophet used to say the following about her, "Fatima is the mother of her father (*Umme Abeeha*)."[27] Secondly, she was the only daughter regarded and revered in the Qur'an and *sunnah* as the leader of all the women. Thirdly, she was the only child of the Prophet whom Allah had purified.[28] Fourthly, through her came the Prophet's eleven descendents and successors. Lastly and most importantly, it was the decree of Allah to gift Fatima al-Zahra the land of Fadak.

The Ahlul Bayt scholars also draw upon Sunni references to solidify their belief that Fadak was indeed a gift to Fatima al-Zahra. For instance, when chapter 17, verse 26 was revealed in the Qur'an,[29] Sunni commentators say that it pertained to the Prophet bestowing Fadak upon his daughter Fatima al-Zahra. Sunni traditionalists narrated that the Prophet asked the Angel Gabriel in reference to, "And render to the kindred their rights" (c. 17:26) the following, "Who are the kinsmen and what is their due?" The Angel Gabriel replied, "Give Fadak to Fatima for it is her due, and whatever is due to Allah and the Prophet out of Fadak also belongs to her, so entrust it to her also."[30]

---

[26] *Sahih al-Muslim, Kitab al-Hibat*, no. 14

[27] *Bihar al-Anwar*, 43:19

[28] *Holy Qur'an*, 33:33

[29] *Holy Qur'an*, 17:26, "And render to the kindred their due rights..."

[30] Narration can be found through al-Bazzaz, Abu Yala, Ibn Abi Hatim, Ibn Marduwayh, and others from Abu Said al-Khudri and through Ibn Marduwayh from Abdullah b. al-Abbas; *al-Mustadrak*, 4:63; *History of Tabari*, 3:3460; *al-Istiab*, 4:1793; *Usud al-Ghabah*, 5:567;

As mentioned earlier, according to both schools of thought, Fadak belonged to the Prophet who then presented it to Fatima al-Zahra.[31] According to the Sunni version of events, after the departure of the Prophet and the succession of Abu Bakr, he (Abu Bakr) was obligated by the Prophet's tradition to seize his (the Prophet's) assets as public property. The Shia version argues that confiscation of Fadak and other properties were unwarranted based on the Qur'an and that Abu Bakr's tradition was unfounded.

According to the teachings of the Ahlul Bayt, Fadak had been in Fatima al-Zahra's possession for four years prior to the death of the Prophet. They also make a strong point that Abu Bakr had known all along that the Prophet gifted Fadak to Fatima al-Zahra because he had been present during the conquest of Khaybar and had known what the Prophet did with Fadak afterwards.

According to both schools of thought, upon becoming caliph, Abu Bakr ousted Fatima's hired residents from the land of Fadak and confiscated the land along with other properties that she owned in Madinah. Fatima immediately went to Abu Bakr to protest the seizures and he dismissed her claim by citing the following tradition of the Prophet, "We, the folk of prophets do not leave bequests; what we leave is for alms."[32]

Fatima al-Zahra employed various means to prove her entitlement to the land. First, she came seeking Fadak as an entitlement of a gift by her father; however, Abu Bakr refused her claim on the account of him hearing from the Prophet that prophets do not leave inheritance. She rebutted his argument by stating that the land was a gift, thus not considered a bequest. After Abu Bakr's continued refusal to relinquish her property, Fatima then requested her right to inheritance according to the Qur'an for which Abu Bakr asked her to bring forth witnesses.

---

al-Tabaqat, 8:192; *al-Isabah*, 4:432

[31] Ali b. Burhanuddin al-Halabi al-Shafi, comp., *Siratu'l-Halabiyya*, p.39

[32] Karmani's commentary, *Sahih al-Bukhari*, 15:4

Some Sunni scholars question as to why Fatima al-Zahra claimed Fadak as her inheritance if it was a gift. The response is that Fatima al-Zahra was compelled to claim her right as an inheritance according to the Qur'an because Abu Bakr would not recognize it as a gift. Besides, if both schools of thought have recorded narrations that Fadak was gifted to Fatima al-Zahra during the life of the Prophet then Abu Bakr's narration does not apply to this case. He had no grounds to claim it as the Prophet's property because it no longer belonged to the Prophet.

According to other reports, Fatima al-Zahra claimed Fadak as being a gift from the Prophet, which Abu Bakr requested witnesses in which Fatima al-Zahra brought forward witnesses.[33] In some accounts, the witnesses were Ali b. Abi Talib, Umme Ayman (the wife of the Prophet), and Rabah, a freed slave of the Prophet.[34] In other accounts, the witnesses were Ali and Umme Ayman.[35] While in others, the witnesses were Ali, Hasan, and Husayn; and in some traditions, Umme Ayman[36] is also included, however Abu Bakr rejected all of these people. In some of the reports, Abu Bakr refused Fatima al-Zahra's witnesses on account of them being her immediate family members. In other reports, he denied her witnesses on account that they fell short of the criteria needed to be witnesses.

In regards to the witnesses, Shia scholars disapprove of Abu Bakr requesting Fatima al-Zahra to bring forth witnesses on account of the following arguments: Fatima's testimony alone should have sufficed, and there was no need for any witnesses on the account of Allah having purified her, which was also extended to Ali, Hasan, and Husayn.[37] In contrast, on a different occasion, Abu Bakr had accepted the testimony of one person, such as Jabir b. Abdullah al-Ansari, so why did he then

---

[33] *Siratul Halabiyya*, p.39

[34] Al-Baladhuri, *More Facts on Fadak*, comments from Futuhul Buldan, p.48

[35] Ibid

[36] Al-Yaqubi, *al-Tarikh*, 3:195-96

[37] *Holy Qur'an*, 33:33

deny Fatima al-Zahra's testimony? The event is recorded in history as follows:

> When the Prophet died, Abu Bakr received some property from al-Ala al-Hadrami. Abu Bakr said to the people, "Whoever has a money claim on the Prophet or was promised something by him should come to us (so that we may pay him his right)." Jabir added, I said (to Abu Bakr), "Allah's Apostle promised me that he would give me this much, and this much, and this much (spreading his hands three times)." Jabir added, "Abu Bakr counted for me and handed me five hundred gold pieces, and then five hundred, and then five hundred (more)."[38]

Many more exceptions to the 'verse of evidence,' (c. 2:282) as recorded in the traditions narrated by the School of the Companions can be seen, such as in the example of Khazima b. Thabit. This individual gave evidence in support of the Prophet in a case concerning the sale of a horse, in which an Arab man had made a claim against the Prophet and his (*Khazima's*) single testimony was considered sufficient, and through this the Prophet gave him the title of "*Dhush Shahadatain*" (the person whose single testimony is equivalent to two people) because he was regarded as being equal to two just witnesses."[39] Thus, again why is it that Abu Bakr could not make an exception for Fatima al-Zahra?

A critical examination into Abu Bakr's narration shows us the reason. Abu Bakr said, "I heard the Messenger saying, 'We do not leave inheritance. What we leave behind is charity.'"[40] The Shia scholars deny such a tradition because it goes against the Qur'anic injunction regarding inheritance[41] and the verses that mention about past prophets inheriting.[42] Nonetheless, Abu Bakr upheld the above quoted alleged

---

[38] *Sahih al-Muslim*, 7:75-76; Ahmad al-Hanbal, *al-Musnad*, 3:307-308

[39] *Sahih al-Bukhari*, 4:24 & 6:146; Abu Dawud, *Sunan*, 3:308

[40] *Sahih al-Muslim*, *Kitab al-Jihad Was`-Siyar*, no. 49

[41] *Holy Qur'an*, 4:7 & 4:33

[42] *Holy Qur'an*, 27:16 & 19:5-6

tradition in the face of Fatima al-Zahra's claim and the clear verses of the Qur'an.

According to Sunni tradition, the hadith Abu Bakr quoted is considered as genuine, since it can be found in what they describe as *sahih* (authentic) books, such as *Sahih al-Bukhari* and *Sahih al-Muslim*, thus making the tradition irrefutable. In addition to their own sources, they also refer to traditions from Shia books on the subject. For example, from one of the major four books of the Shia, *al-Kafi* by Shaykh al-Kulayni, Imam Jafar as-Sadiq has been quoted as saying that the Prophet said, "...And the *ulama* (Islamic scholars) are the heirs of the *anbiya* (prophets); and the *anbiya* did not leave *dinars* and *dirhams* (money) as inheritance; but they do leave knowledge. Therefore, whosoever takes knowledge has taken a great portion."[43] In addition, in order to justify that Abu Bakr acted rightfully in denying Fadak to Fatima al-Zahra, Sunni scholars also cite the following tradition mentioned in the Shia books, "Women do not inherit anything of the land or fixed property."[44] They also cite the following hadith, "They (women) will get the value of the bricks, the building, the wood and the bamboo. As for the land and the fixed property, they will get no inheritance from that."[45]

However, the Shia scholars do not remain silent when hadith are cited from their books in order to justify actions taken against Fatima al-Zahra. The scholars explain that the tradition regarding the *"anbiya* (prophets) not leaving inheritance" is not in reference to the traditional inheritance of heirs; but rather, it is in the context of inheriting the spirit and knowledge of Islam. Moreover, Shia scholars point not only towards the Qur'anic verses that mention prophets inheriting, such as Prophet Sulayman inheriting from Prophet Dawud,[46] but also, that Prophet Muhammad himself inherited from his father. Abdullah b. Abdul

---

[43] Al-Kulayni, *Al-Kafi*, 1:42

[44] Al-Kulayni, *Al-Kafi*, 7:127

[45] *Bihar al-Anwar*, 104:351

[46] *Holy Qur'an*, 27:16

Muttalib (the Prophet's father) left to Aminah (the Prophet's mother) a legacy of five colored camels and a small flock of sheep which was inherited by the Prophet.[47]

In regards to the tradition that women are not permitted to inherit land or property, Shia scholars say that the tradition only applies to the inheritance of a wife from her husband. Thus, it is not applicable to Abu Bakr's action in denying Fatima her right to inherit from her father. Plus they argue that had Abu Bakr's tradition been accurate then Fatima al-Zahra and Ali b. Abi Talib would have known about it for several reasons. First, they were closest to the Prophet and such a tradition would have affected them both. In addition, Ali would have certainly been aware of the hadith since he was the "gateway" of Islamic knowledge. The Prophet used to refer to Ali as, "I am the city of knowledge and Ali is its gate." Secondly, they would have never come forward with such a claim if the tradition was accurate.

For the most part, Shia theologians and historians present undisputable arguments and we see that in all accounts, Fadak was rightfully the property of Fatima al-Zahra as it had been gifted to her; and if we presume that it was not gifted to her, then still, if analyzed objectively, one would conclude that she had a right to claim it as an inheritance. By virtue of Fatima al-Zahra's stature, her testimony, coupled with the Qur'an, take precedence over Abu Bakr's tradition and position. Thus, to justify Abu Bakr's action falls short before Fatima al-Zahra's grandeur. Although various reasons are cited by others to justify Abu Bakr's claim, but the main intent behind the confiscation of Fadak is closely tied to the usurpation of the Islamic leadership after the Prophet, and thus the underlying reason for the confiscation of Fadak was to deny Ali and Fatima al-Zahra any economic power which would have enabled them to forge a greater stand against Abu Bakr's leadership.

---

[47] Tabaqat b. Sa'd, part 1:39; Moulana Shibli al-Noumani, *Siratan Nabi*, 1:122

Stand Against Imam Ali

Since power remained firm in the hands of the Quraysh group, and they limited their ranks to those who had refused to pay allegiance to Ali b. Abi Talib, Ali bore the brunt of this group's enmity.

The only individuals who could move up in the ranks were those who had refused to pay allegiance to Ali - people such as al-Mugheerah b. Shu'bah, Amr b. al-Aas, Abu Musa al-Ashari, Sa'd b. Abil Waqqas, Mu'awiyah b. Abu Sufyan, Abu Huraira, Utbah b. Abu Sufyan, Sa'ed b. al-Aas, and al-Waleed b. Uqbah.

For forty years, the leadership who bore deep animosity towards Ali, forced mercenary speakers to ascend the pulpit and curse him in addition to the daughter of the Holy Prophet and their children, Hasan and Husayn.[48] If anyone ventured outside of this jurisdiction and tried to mention the virtues of Ali, they were warned that that was a crime punishable by death. This forced scholars, such as Hasan al-Basri to refer to the fourth caliph, Ali, as "Abu Zaynab (the father of Zaynab)." Their vindictiveness continued despite the agreed upon saying of Prophet Muhammad, narrated by both Sunni and Shia that, "O Ali, no one likes you except a believer, and no one hates you except a hypocrite."[49]

Ali was of such a high status in the sight of the Holy Prophet that when *Surah al-Bara'at* (*The Disavowal*, also known as *al-Tawbah* (*The Repentance*)) was revealed, the Prophet sent Abu Bakr as the *amir* (caravan leader) of the Hajj to recite it (and thus to offer the Quraysh a stern warning). However while on the way to Mecca, Abu Bakr was intercepted by Ali b. Abi Talib through the Divine decree given by Allah to Prophet Muhammad. The Angel Gabriel instructed the Prophet with Allah's order, "No one delivers on your behalf except yourself or a man

---

[48] *Al-Kamil fil-Tarikh*, 5:42

[49] *Sahih al-Tirmidhi*, 2:301; *Sahih al-Nisai*, 2:271; *Sahih b. Majah*, p. 12; Abu Nuaym, *Hiliyat al-Awiya*, 4:185

from you." Afterwards the Prophet commented, "Ali is from me, and I am from him, and no one delivers (the revelation) except me or Ali."[50]

In reality, the intense opposition towards Ali b. Abi Talib proves that without a doubt, the Quraysh group did recognize that Ali was bound to succeed the Prophet. What other reason could they possibly have had for ritualizing invocations against him? If nothing else, he was a companion with the highest recorded caliber of service to Islam and the Prophet. He was the father of the Prophet's grandchildren and he was never known to have committed any wrong act. Although he maintained that the caliphate should have gone to him, he did not raise arms, and he only assumed the caliphate after the institution itself had crumbled. Had he been only a mere contender, the ruling powers would have exiled him - even annihilated him, just as they did to companions such as Abu Dharr al-Ghifari.

Instead, the Quraysh group was more concerned with assassinating the character of Ali, and in hindsight, their propaganda campaign points all the more clearly to the reality that they were trying to cover up the Prophet's command that Ali was to be his successor.

In the end, this intense hatred turned into violent bloodshed when the wife of the Prophet, Lady Aishah, despite having been warned by the Prophet not to transgress against Ali,[51] mobilized 30,000 fighters and marched from Madinah to Basra in a confrontation known as the Battle of Camel (Battle of Jamal). Lady Aishah instigated the first battle in Islam in which Muslims raised swords against one another, and as a result, she caused the death of 20,000 Muslims from her side and another 500 from the defense of Ali's army.

Following her lead, Mu'awiyah also took arms against Ali during his caliphate resulting in the Battle of Siffeen, in which 70,000 Muslims lost their lives. Indeed, she did not take heed to what the Prophet had said to

---

[50] *Musnad Ahmad b. al-Hanbal*, 4:164; *Kanz al-Ummal*, 6:153

[51] *Musnad Ahmad*, 6:52; *Al-Imamah wal-Siyasah*, 1163; *Tarikh al-Tabari*, 4:469

Ali, "May God fight the one who fights you and may God be hostile to the one who is hostile towards you."[52]

---

[52] *Usud al-Ghabah*, 2:154; *Al-Isabah*, 1:501

Chapter 6
Transition of the Group

﴿وَمَثَلُ كَلِمَةٍ خَبِيثَةٍ كَشَجَرَةٍ خَبِيثَةٍ اجْتُثَّتْ مِن فَوْقِ
الأَرْضِ مَا لَهَا مِن قَرَارٍ﴾

*And the parable of an evil word is that of an evil tree: It is torn up
by the root from the surface of the earth: it has no stability.*

Holy Qur'an, 14:26

The Cursed Tree

Since the advent of the revelation of the Qur'an, the Bani Umayyah
spearheaded a calculated fight against Islam. Having received full
knowledge of their evil traits through revelation, the Holy Prophet
repeatedly cursed them,[1] specifically Abu Sufyan b. Harb.[2] Even Allah,
referring to them metaphorically in the Qur'an cursed them when He
said, "And the cursed tree in the Qur'an..." (c. 17:60) Both Sunni and Shia
commentators agree that this "cursed tree" is none other than the Bani
Umayyah.[3]

Generation after generation, they perpetuated their hatred towards
the religion of Islam and their attempts to overcome it. Initially, in
Mecca and Madinah, Abu Sufyan and his son Mu'awiyah severely
tormented the Muslims. The attacks by Abu Sufyan led the reputable
Sunni historian, Ibn Abd al-Birr to declare that, "Abu Sufyan was a

---

[1] Al-Hakim al-Hasakani, *Al-Mustadrak*, 4:480

[2] *Al-Isabah*, 2:38; *Usd al-Ghabah*, 3:76

[3] Al-Suyuti, *Al-Durr al-Manthur*; Al-Bayhaqi, *Al-Dalail*

shelter for all the hypocrites who were against the Muslims after he embraced Islam and what is correct (to say) is that he did not embrace Islam, but rather he unwillingly surrendered to the Muslims."[4] His animosity prevailed some fourteen years after his "conversion" when he kicked the grave of the martyred uncle of the Prophet, Hamzah, and mocked him saying, "O *Aba Imarah*, the issue [Islamic leadership] which you fought against us with the sword is now in the hands of our children who are playing with it."[5]

Mu'awiyah, on the other hand, took a less vocal stance during his caliphate and simply killed those prominent companions of the Prophet who disagreed with his totalitarian policies. Among the souls whom he escorted out of the life of this world were the grandson of the Prophet, Imam Hasan, Hijr b. Uday, Malik al-Ashtar, Muhammad b. Abu Bakr, Ammar b. Yasir, Abd al-Rahman b. Abu Bakr, and Sa'd b. Abu al-Waqqas.[6]

Mu'awiyah continued his mayhem by killing many of the Ansar and memorizers of the Holy Qur'an. Mu'awiyah's son Yazid continued the trend years later by murdering the other grandson of the Prophet, Imam Husayn in the tragic massacre at Karbala in the year 61 AH, in which he then took the women and children of the Prophet's household captive and dishonored them by parading them through Iraq and Syria. Yazid broadened his reign of terror and havoc by allowing his soldiers to rape the women and pillage the city of Madinah in the year 62 AH and topped his rule of tyranny with setting out to destroy the Ka'abah in the year 63 AH.

Anyone who indulges in such vile practices should not only have been banned from leading the Islamic government, but should have also been ostracized from the nation. Yet, despite the inclinations of the Bani Umayyah and the curse of Allah upon them, both the first and the

---

[4] Ibn Abd al-Birr, *Al-Istiab*, 2:690

[5] Ibn Abil Hadid, *Sharh Nahjul Balaghah*

[6] Ibn al-Atheer 3:440; *Al-Istiab*, p. 839; Ibn Hajar, *Al-Isabah*, 3:384

second caliphs involved them in their power structure and exposed the ummah to their treachery.

They made Uthman a senior aide (vizier) and made use of others, such as Mu'awiyah, Utbah, Yazid, Sa'eed b. al-Aas, al-Waleed b. Uqbah, and Uttab b. Usayd, while other worthy men went unrepresented.

Ironically, at one time, the first caliph confided to al-Mugheerah b. Shu'bah his fear that the Bani Umayyah posed a serious threat to Islam and said, "By Allah, Bani Umayyah will cause Islam to become one-eyed."[7] Yet ironically, Umar privileged people from the Bani Umayyah over others in his government. When Mu'awiyah was only 18 years old, Umar appointed him governor of Syria, although Umar himself had refused to join the dispatch of Usama b. Zayd upon the order of the Holy Prophet on the pretext that Usama was only 18; and he also objected to the caliphate of Ali b. Abi Talib because Ali was too young - 33 years old.[8] In response to the criticism that Mu'awiyah was too young to govern, Umar retorted, "Are you criticizing me for appointing him? I heard the Prophet say about Mu'awiyah, 'God, make a guide (*hadi*), a guided one (*mahdi*), and guide the people by him.'"[9]

Umar even knighted some well-known enemies of the Prophet and Islam with honored titles. Abu Sufyan was given the title of "*Sayyid Quraysh* (Leader of the Quraysh)," while he called Mu'awiyah, "*Kisra al-Arab*" - "*kisra*" being the word for a noble Persian king, and he called Hind, the mother of Mu'awiyah, "*Karemat Quraysh* (the Honorable Lady of Quraysh)." In reality, reports on Hind say otherwise about her honor as the report according to Ibn al-Katheer shows:

> In the Battle of Uhud, Hind, the mother of Mu'awiyah who was the wife of Abu Sufyan was butchering the martyrs of the Muslims -

---

[7] Ibn Sa'd, *Al-Tabaqat al-Kubra*, 7:78

[8] Ibn Abil Hadid, *Sharh Nahjul-Balaghah*, 3:115

[9] Ibn Katheer, *Sunan al-Tirmidhi*; *Al-Bidayah wal-Nihayah*, 8:120

including Hamzah the uncle of the Prophet - and amputating their limbs.[10]

Is it possible that someone who had committed such horrendous acts be entitled as an "honorable woman?" Little evidence exists to indicate that Hind was sincere when she later embraced Islam. The Bani Umayyah remained as the Qur'an had described them - "the Cursed Tree."

How easily did the Quraysh group forget the admonitions of the Holy Qur'an and the Noble Prophet, and yet they were to become the ruling dynasty of the Muslim world. Instead of the hadith of the Prophet warning the people against Bani Umayyah - or even the words of Umar b. al-Khattab warning himself against them - an exorbitant amount of false hadith began to appear claiming the high status of the Bani Umayyah in the sight of Allah. Indeed, the "evil word" of the "cursed tree" had begun to spread its roots.

---

[10] Ibn Katheer, 4:42

Chapter 7
Prohibition of Transcribing the Hadith

﴿بِالْبَيِّنَاتِ وَالزُّبُرِ وَأَنزَلْنَا إِلَيْكَ الذِّكْرَ لِتُبَيِّنَ لِلنَّاسِ مَا
نُزِّلَ إِلَيْهِمْ وَلَعَلَّهُمْ يَتَفَكَّرُونَ﴾

*(We sent them) with Clear Signs and Scriptures; and We have sent
down unto thee (also) the Message; that you may explain clearly to
men what is sent for them, and that they may reflect.*

Holy Qur'an, 16:44

Without a doubt, the art of writing separates the truth from falsehood,
maintains agreements, and reminds people of what has passed and many
other important things. Even during the pre-Islamic era, writing was a
rare but honored skill. According to Ibn Sa'd, "The accomplished among
them in the time before Islam were those who wrote Arabic, mastered
swimming, and mounted archery."[1] Various schools in Mecca, Madinah
and Taif taught the difficult art of the Arabic script.

When Islam came, its teachings prioritized writing and the
advancement of knowledge and imagery of books and writing permeate
the verses of the Qur'an. One of the first verses which Allah revealed
was, "[He] Who taught by the use of the pen,"[2] thus making the pen as
an instrument used for a binding oath, such as in *Surah al-Qalam*, "By the
pen and by what they write."[3] Therefore, despite the difficulties of

---

[1] Ibn Sa'd, *Al-Tabaqat al-Kubra*, 3:2 91

[2] *Holy Qur'an*, 96:4

[3] *Holy Qur'an*, 68:1

writing at that time, gradually the *jahiliyyah* (pre-Islamic) society slowly became literate.

After establishing the mosque in Madinah, one of the priorities of the Prophet had was to appoint a teacher, Abdullah b. Sa'd al-Aas to teach reading and writing. This skill was so important that the Prophet even allowed some of the captives taken during the Battle of Badr to earn their freedom in exchange for teaching ten Muslims how to read and write.[4] Between forty-three and forty-five scribes recorded the revelations of the Qur'an at the Prophet's request, and in addition, he would constantly urge the people to "write (*uktubu*)"[5] and "document (*qayyidu*),"[6] and would advise, "Help yourself to memorize by writing."[7]

Most significant, the Prophet commanded that his hadith (sayings and actions) be written down. He instructed the Muslims, "Write everything that comes out of my mouth, for by the One whose Hands my soul is in, nothing comes from it except the truth."[8] Abu Bakr narrates from the Holy Prophet that, "Whoever writes down a piece of knowledge from me or a hadith will receive *ajr* (reward) as long as it (the writing) exists."[9] A companion, Abdullah b. al-Aas used to put everything the Prophet said in writing to such an extent that some companions of the Prophet ordered him to stop doing so because they felt that the Prophet was just a human being whose utterance should not be recorded. He consulted with the Prophet and the Prophet replied, "Yes, write down everything that I say."[10] Similarly, on the authority of Rafi b. Khadij we read that:

---

[4] Ibn Sa'd, *Al-Tabaqat al-Kubra*, 2:22

[5] *Sunan al-Tirmidhi*, 4:146, hadith 2805

[6] *Mustadrak al-Hakim*, 1:106

[7] *Sunan al-Tirmidhi*, 4:145, hadith 2804

[8] *Al-Mustadrak ala al-Sahihayn*, I 5:106; *Musnad Ahmad*, 2:162; *Jami Bayan al-Ilm*, 1:71

[9] *Kanz al-Ummal*, 5:237, hadith 4845

[10] Rashid Ridha, *Tafseer al-Manar*, 10:766

The Prophet of Allah passed by us one day and we were talking. He said, "What are you talking about?" We replied, "What we heard from you." He said, "So talk about it, but whoever deliberately attributes false statements to me reserves his place in the hell-fire," and then the people stopped talking. The Prophet asked why they were not talking anymore, and they replied that they had stopped talking because of his serious words. He said, "I did not say not to talk. I said, 'speak, but speak the truth.' I only ask you not to attribute false statements to me." They said to him, "O Prophet of God, we hear things from you, should we write them down?" He said, "Yes, by all means, write them down. By thy Lord, everything that comes out of my mouth is the truth."[11]

In addition, the Prophet emphasized the transmission of his teachings through other means. He repeated twice saying, "Therefore, the witness must inform the absent,"[12] regarding those who were not present to hear his words. He also encouraged the Muslims to memorize his sayings in order to transmit them and as a way to verify their authenticity. In this regard, the Prophet would say, "Whoever memorizes and conveys forty hadith from my tradition, I will admit him into my intercession on the Day of Judgment,"[13] and "Whoever from my ummah memorizes forty hadith, Allah will raise him on the Day of Judgment as a scholar."[14]

Despite all this significance and attention given to recording the hadith of the Prophet, during the reign of the first three caliphs, the Muslims were absolutely forbidden from recording any hadith.[15] In the words of Lady Aishah:

---

[11] Ibn Uday, *Taqaid al-Ilm*, 73; *Al-Kamil*, 1:36

[12] *Sahih al-Muslim*, 5:108; *Sunan b. Majah*, 1:85; *Al-Tirmidhi*, 2:152; *Mustadrak al-Hakim*, 3:174, and others

[13] *Kanz al-Ummal*, 10:158, hadith 28817

[14] *Kanz al-Ummal*, 10:158, hadith 28818, and others

[15] Despite being forbidden from doing so, the followers of Ahlul Bayt continued to record the hadith.

My father collected the hadith of the Messenger of Allah and they numbered five hundred. He spent the night turning back and forth. He saddened me and I said to him, "Are you turning around because of pain, or because of bad news which you have received?" In the morning, he said to me, "Bring me the hadith of the Prophet which I have left with you." I brought him all the hadith. At this point, he asked for fire and burned all the hadith in the fire. I said to him, "Why do you burn these hadith?" He said, "I fear that I will die while I have these hadith. I took them from the man I trusted, but maybe some hadith are not his or maybe the sayings are not authentic."[16]

The excuse proffered in the above quote is that the hadith might not have been authentic. However, Abu Bakr could hardly have had reason to doubt traditions that he heard with his own ears and from other companions whom he himself says he trusted.

This position becomes even more difficult to accept when coupled with the idea subsequently introduced by scholars, such as Ibn Hajar that Allah did not allow the companions to lie or make mistakes!

In later times, in order to support Abu Bakr's action, a false saying was cited on the authority of Abu Sa'id al-Khudri stating, "Whoever took from me other than the Qur'an and wrote it down, let him erase it."[17] Aside from the fact that this hadith contradicts previous hadith in which the Prophet ordered the Muslims to write down his traditions and the spirit of the Holy Qur'an which encourages writing, if this hadith was authentic then Abu Bakr would certainly have been aware of it and would never have narrated any hadith.

To placate the people, Abu Bakr said, "Between us and you is the book of Allah, so follow the lawful in it and refrain from the prohibited." Across the board, both Shia and Sunni scholars believe that the Qur'an alone does not suffice for a comprehensive explanation of Islam and it is

---

[16] *Tadhkirat al-Huffaz,* 1:5; *Hujiyat al-Sunnah,* p. 394

[17] Al-Nawawi; *Sharh Sahih al-Muslim,* 17-18; *Musnad Ahmad* 3:12

in need of the Prophet's explanation as a supplement. Even more, the verses of the Qur'an fall into many categories, such as *mujmal* (having equal possibilities) and *mubayan* (clearly recognized); *muhkam* (fundamental or basic) and *mutashabih* (vague); *aam* (general) and *khass* (specific); and *naasikh* (abrogating) and *mansukh* (abrogated). It is for this reason that Allah did not leave the Muslims without a guide to the proper interpretation thereof. Allah says in the Holy Qur'an, "Whoever obeys the Prophet has obeyed Allah,"[18] and "Your Companion (Muhammad) errs not, nor is he led astray, nor does he speaks of his own inclination."[19] Similarly, the Prophet said, "By Allah, I have commanded and admonished and prohibited things, and just like the Qur'an, you have to follow what I say,"[20] and "Verily, I have been given the Qur'an and something equivalent to it [the hadith]."[21] One of his final injunctions to the Muslims was, "I am leaving among you the Book of Allah and my family (*itrati*);" "*itrati*," also refers to the hadith of the Prophet and his family.

In a hadith narrated in the Sunni books, the Messenger of Allah prophesized:

> It is imminent that a man will narrate from me while leaning on his couch and then he will say, 'Between us and between you is the Book of Allah. When we find something permissible in it, we will follow it, and when we find something impermissible in it, we will refrain from it.'[22]

Umar continued the hadith precedent of Abu Bakr during his caliphate. However, at one point, he consulted the companions of the Prophet

---

[18] *Holy Qur'an*, 4:80

[19] *Holy Qur'an*, 53:2-4

[20] Ibn Hazm, *Al-Ahkam*, 1:159

[21] *Musnad Ahmad*, 4:131

[22] *Musnad Ahmad*, 4:132; *Sunan b. Majah*, 1:6, hadith 12; *Sunan Abu Dawood*, 4:200, hadith 4604; *Sunan al-Bayhaqi*, 9:331

about recording hadith and they encouraged him to do so. After considering the matter for a month, Umar then declared:

> My intention was to record hadith but then I realized that some people (nations) before you kept writing down the sayings of their prophets, and kept reading them; as a result, they forgot the book of Allah (their scriptures). I fear that the same will happen if I order you to document the sayings of the Prophet, or if I do it myself. I do not want to make the Book of Allah a victim here because of the hadith; nothing has precedence over the Book of Allah. [23]

He then wrote to the Ansar, "Whoever has anything should erase it."[24] Even afterwards Umar decreed, "These (the hadith of the Prophet) are just like the Jewish scripts (*mushnat*), and they must be burnt."[25] He then gathered all of the hadith written on leather, tablets, and pieces of wood and ordered them to be burnt.[26]

However, it is important to note that the People of the Book (Jews and Christians) did not neglect their scriptures (Holy Revelations) in favor of the sayings of their prophets [hadith]. Their problem was not that they were overly fastidious in transcribing the sayings of their prophets. Instead, they neglected almost all of the traditions of their prophets, as well as the commands of their Divinely sent books (i.e. the Tawrah). They also refused to follow the successors that their prophets named, such as Asif b. Barkhiyah, the successor of Prophet Sulayman, and Yushaa, the successor of Prophet Musa.

As agreed by both schools of thought, the Messenger of Allah forewarned that the Muslims would follow the pattern of previous generations when he said, "You will follow the footsteps and tradition of

---

[23] *Kanzl Ummal*, 10, hadith 29474

[24] *Taqid al-Ilm*, 49; *Hujjiyat al-Sunnah*, 3:95

[25] Ibn Sa'd, *Tabaqat al-Kubra*, 1:140

[26] *Kanz al-Ummal*, 5:239

the nations before you step by step."[27] Since the first three caliphs enforced the policy of not recording the sayings, fabricators such as Ka'ab al-Ahbar[28] and Tamim b. Aus al-Dari[29] flourished and spread thousands of false hadith, forever affecting Islam.

Furthermore, fearing that they would spread the sayings of the Prophet outside Madinah, the second caliph summoned many of the prominent companions, such as Abdullah b. Hudaafah, Ibn Masud,[30] Abu Dardah,[31] Abu Dharr al-Ghifari,[32] and Uqbaah b. Aamir to Madinah and rebuked them saying, "What is it that you have done! You spread the hadith of the Prophet in other places. You have to stay here (in Madinah) and you will not depart or separate from me as long as I live." Thus, they were confined to Madinah until Umar was assassinated.[33] Al-Shibi says that the Muhajireen from the Quraysh despised Umar for confining them to Madinah, so that they would not spread the hadith elsewhere. The situation reached to a point that some of the men would ask permission to accompany the *ghazw* (military dispatch) and Umar would tell them, "No, you had your share with the Prophet, and you had enough reward

---

[27] *Al-Mu'jam ul-Kabeer*, 7:281; *Tafseer al-Qurtubi*, 7:273

[28] His full name is Ka'ab b. Mate'ah al-Himyari, a prominent Jewish rabbi from Yemen. He accepted Islam during the reign of Umar b. al-Khattab and migrated from Yemen to Syria. Mu'awiyah favored him and made him one of his important right hand aids and advisors. He is one of the main sources of the Israelite folklore that infected the Islamic tradition and was known for his lies. He died during the reign of Uthman in 32 AH.

[29] Tamim b. Aus al-Dari was a prominent Christian monk in Palestine. He embraced Islam in 9 AH. He was the first person to introduce story telling in the mosque during the reign of Umar al-Khattab and it was only during Imam Ali's reign that he put an end to it. He infiltrated Islamic tradition with unsubstantiated Israelite stories and died in the year 40 AH.

[30] *Mustadrak al-Hakim*, 1:110; *Tarikh Abu Zarah*, 270

[31] Ibid

[32] Ibid

[33] *Kanz al-Ummal*, 10, hadith 29479

for that, so today it is better for you that you do not see the world and for the world not to see you either."[34]

In contrast, others who were not known for their honesty in conveying the hadith of the Prophet, such as al-Waleed b. Uqbah, Hanbal b. Abu Sufyan, and Abdullah b. Abi Sarh were permitted to travel wherever they wanted, even to the conquered lands of Iraq and Persia. However, those who were known for their integrity in transmitting the hadith of the Prophet were forced to remain behind.

Unlike Abu Bakr who expressed fear that the hadith he possessed were not authentic, Umar argued that the hadith should be destroyed because the people might follow them instead of the Qur'an or that they might confuse them with the Qur'an. However, the true hadith hardly led people away from the Qur'an. In fact, the hadith contain an explanation of the Qur'an itself and the more people know about the hadith, the more one would heed to the Qur'an. Allah assigned the Prophet to "make clear to humankind what has been sent down to them,"[35] hence the hadith are extremely vital to understanding the Qur'an.

Similarly, the fear that people might mix up the Qur'an and the hadith is also difficult to understand, since even the average modern reader can readily distinguish between the text of the Qur'an and that of a hadith. The style of the Qur'an is inimitable among human beings and the Qur'an itself says that it is a miracle, and challenges human beings to produce one verse like it - a challenge that the Prophet never issued for his hadith. Such a fear, were it genuine, would imply a severe lack of confidence in the reasoning abilities of the *sahabahs* (companions) who had the additional advantage of hearing the Prophet himself speak.

Muslim analysts believe that the real reason why there was a calculated ploy to prevent the hadith from being recorded was that there were innumerable hadith about the virtues of the household of the

---

[34] Ibn al-Atheer, *Al-Kamil fi al-Tarikh*, 3:180-181

[35] *Holy Qur'an*, 16:44

Prophet and their right to the leadership after the Holy Prophet's death. Had these sayings circulated in written form amongst the predominant *sahih* books then they would have undermined the political legitimacy of the first three caliphs.

As a result, the sad reality developed that, although, the hadith are second only to the Qur'an in Islamic legislation, many authentic sayings of Prophet Muhammad were lost, while many others were forged. The situation degenerated to the level where Mu'awiyah b. Abu Sufyan ordered Kab al-Ahbar to sit in the mosque and invent hadith to read to the people, and no one could disprove what he said because no written sources existed among those masses. It was not until the time of the Umayyah caliph, Umar b. Abd al-Aziz (99 AH) that Muslims were allowed, for a short but unsuccessful period, to record the hadith.[36]

Anyone who tried to compile the hadith of the Prophet faced severe punishment and this state of affair lasted for more than a century - spanning from the periods of the first four[37] caliphs thru to the Bani Umayyah dynasty and until the time of Abu Ja'far al-Mansur of the Abbasid dynasty. Ironically, Mu'awiyah told the people, "Narrate less from the Prophet, and if you want to mention a hadith from him, say what used to be said about him during the time of Umar."[38]

In reality, the policy of not writing hadith took form right before the death of the Prophet when Umar prevented the Prophet from writing his will while the Messenger was on his deathbed, as recorded in prominent Sunni sources, Umar proclaimed that, "The Book of Allah is enough for us."[39]

---

[36] The writing of the hadith was short-lived because the reign of Umar b. Abd al-Aziz lasted for only two years.

[37] Although Imam Ali removed the ban on writing the hadith; nonetheless, it was not enough time to take full effect because his reign lasted for only four years and nine months.

[38] *Kanz al-Ummal*, 10:291; Ibn Abil Hadid, *Sharh Nahjul-Balaghah*, 1:360; *Tarikh Abi Zaah*, p. 270

[39] *Sahih al-Bukhari*; *Bab Marad al-Nabi*; *Ketab al-Marda wa al-Tib*, 7:9

Chapter 8
Legacy of the Quraysh on the Hadith

﴿وَقُلْ جَاءَ الْحَقُّ وَزَهَقَ الْبَاطِلُ إِنَّ الْبَاطِلَ كَانَ زَهُوقًا﴾

Truth has arrived, and falsehood has perished; verily falsehood by its nature perishes.

Holy Qur'an, 17:81

The critical influence of the Quraysh group was not confined to the temporary prohibition of the compilation of hadith. This group and the Bani Umayyah came and went, however the results of their propaganda tactics survive until today in the invented practices that have found their way into the books of hadith.

Under the employment of the Bani Umayyah, individuals such as Abu Huraira al-Dusi and al-Mugheerah b. Shu'bah composed stories ridiculing the household of the Prophet and exaggerating other companions. They even attributed some false hadith to Imam Ali. As a result, the sources of Islamic *shariah* (legal law) and legislation became tainted which lead to many people within the ummah becoming misinformed.

Some Muslims believe that if one rejects any hadith narrated in the six books of hadith called the *Sahih as-Sittah* (the six authentic books of hadith), then they are actually rejecting their faith. Few people realize that belief in the validity of these six *sahih* hadith books is not a prerequisite for faith and that another option does exist.

Where did all of these fabricated hadith come from? A major source is the man whom Umar b. al-Khattab accused of stealing the wealth of the Muslims and called him "the enemy of Allah and the enemy of the Book of Allah"[1] and that man was Abu Huraira, who is known to have narrated over 5,700 hadith. In fact, in regards to him, Umar said, "Most likely because of the abundance of the hadith you have delivered, you are lying about the Prophet."[2] Abu Huraira used to tell stories in which the Prophet would say absurd things and when the Muslims stared at him dumbfounded, he would affirm, "I believe in this hadith, and so do Abu Bakr and Umar." By his own statement, he was implying that no one else had faith to believe in his narrations![3]

Abu Huraira was not the only person who composed his own hadith and attributed the sayings to Prophet Muhammad. Another prominent storyteller was Amr b. al-Aas.[4] For example, Amr b. al-Aas narrates that when Lady Aishah was asked who was the closest person to the heart of the Prophet, she said, "My father." When asked who else, she said, "Umar," and then after him, she named other people.[5] However, Lady Aishah had always maintained that amongst men, the closest person to the Prophet was Ali b. Abi Talib, and that amongst the women it was his daughter, Lady Fatima al-Zahra.[6]

Sunni scholars who carefully examine the *sahih* books would automatically question the authenticity of some of the problematic hadith. Of course, had the Bani Umayyah not begun the practice of forging their own hadith, then the entire science of hadith classification

---

[1] Ibn al-Atheer, *Al-Bidayah wal-Nihayah*, 8:116

[2] Ibn Abil Hadid, *Sharh Nahjul-Balaghah*, 1:360

[3] *Sahih al-Muslim*, 4:1857, hadith 2388

[4] Amr b. al-Aas was one of the most cunning figures in Arab history. He is known for ridiculing and deriding the Prophet. The Holy Qur'an says about him, "For he who hates you, he will be cut off from prosterity (children)."(c. 108:3) He was cursed by the Prophet when he was seen singing and drinking alcohol. Mu'awiyah appointed him to be the governor of Egypt and it was he who fought against Imam Ali in the Battle of Siffeen in 37 AH. He died in Egypt in 43 AH.

[5] *Sahih al-Muslim*, 4:1856, hadith 2384

[6] *Sunan al-Tirmidi*, 5:362

may never have developed. Nevertheless, since they did, the science of hadith classification was developed.

One of the primary principles, which both Sunni and Shia scholars use in the science of hadith, is that if one narrator in a chain of narrators is unreliable then all of his hadiths are meaningless.[7] In this case, why did the fables of Abu Huraira, and those that insulted the Prophet, remain in the *sahih* books? By their own inclusion of a few shortsighted narrators, these false and fabricated hadiths affected Muslim thought forever.

Hadith of the "Ten People Guaranteed Paradise"

One of the most infamous hadith a fabrication is referred to as, "Ten People Guaranteed Paradise (*al-Asharah Mubashsharah bil-Jannah*)."

According to this hadith the "ten people guaranteed Paradise" are: (1) Abu Bakr b. Abi Qahafah (2) Umar b. al-Khattab (3) Uthman b. al-Affan (4) Talha b. Ubaydillah (5) Zubayr b. al-Awam (6) Abd al-Rahman b. Auf (7) Sa'd b. Abi Waqqas (8) Abdullah b. Masoud (9) Abu Obaydah b. al-Jarrah and (10) Ali b. Abi Talib. Collectively granting them all paradise puts us in a great dilemma because many of these individuals are known for their questionable character.

To begin with, only al-Tirmidhi includes this hadith, whereas al-Bukhari, al-Muslim, and al-Dhahabi all reject it.[8] It behooves us to ask why the other prominent hadith recorders did not mention this hadith, since being guaranteed Paradise assures that their course of life was traveled correctly. Then who narrated this "hadith?" Near the top of the chain of narrators lies Sa'ed b. Zayd, the son-in-law of the second caliph - a man who refused to pay allegiance to Imam Ali during his caliphate.

Another point to consider is that those guaranteed Paradise should include those who sacrificed their lives and properties in the path of

---

[7] Al-Imam al-Nawawi, *Al-Taqrib*

[8] Al-Dhahabi, *Mizan al-Itedaal*

Allah, so why were not the hundreds of martyrs and companions included in this hadith? For example, the "Leader of the Martyrs (*Sayyid al-Shuhada*)," Hamzah, the uncle of the Holy Prophet is not included in this hadith, nor are any of the Ansar whom the Holy Prophet constantly praised.

Above that, to guarantee Paradise to Talha, Zubayr, Abd al-Rahman b. Auf, and Uthman b. al-Affan would bring about a problem for several reasons. First, Talha, Zubayr, and Abd al-Rahman b. Auf used to call Uthman a "*fasiq*" (indecent), and they eventually revolted against him during his caliphate. In addition, Talha and Zubayr pressed for a civil war by supporting and joining Lady Aishah in the Battle of the Camel, in which both of them were killed in the battle. Secondly, Uthman and Abd al-Rahman b. Auf (whom Umar nicknamed "the Pharaoh of this nation"[9]), after a falling out, did not speak to one another until death. Furthermore, after Uthman's assassination, the Muslims were so angry with Uthman that they did not allow for his body to be buried in al-Baqi cemetery; hence, his remains were buried in the Jewish cemetery of Kokab.[10] He remained buried there until Mu'awiyah came to power and included him in the common cemetery of al-Baqi, in Madinah. To add, Sa'd b. Abi al-Waqqas refused to pay allegiance to Imam Ali even when the rest of the ummah accepted him as their fourth caliph. Nevertheless, many Muslim leaders still cite this fabricated hadith, and many Muslims embrace it unquestioningly.

Umar b. al-Khattab

Many of the fabricated hadith were introduced to provide religious legitimacy for the government of the caliphs. In fact, that could be seen as the primary motive for inventing hadith. For this reason, many posthumous narrations are recorded in praise of Umar b. al-Khattab;

---

[9] Ibn Qutaybah, *Al-Imamah wal-Siyasah*, 24

[10] Ibn Abd al-Birr, *Al-Estiaab*

some of which are attributed to the Prophet having said them, others to Imam Ali, and some are attributed to various companions.

However, almost all of these hadith are flawed as either they contradict the Qur'an, the *sunnah* or other established facts, or one or more of their narrators are known to be unreliable, according to the standards of recognizing the hadith in the Sunni tradition.

Virtually all of the fabricated sayings in praise of Umar appeared during the time of Bani Umayyah, particularly during the rule of Mu'awiyah b. Abu Sufyan, for obvious reasons, since the Bani Umayyah was attempting to consolidate their rule. In contrast, most of the reliable hadith about Umar that appeared during his lifetime and have been included in the Sunni books are not overly favorable for him.

Umar is recorded to have said about himself, "All people are more knowledgeable than Umar, even the housewives."[11] He asks, "Doesn't it surprise you that your leader erred and a lady in his audience corrected him?"[12] He also spoke about himself saying, "All the people are more knowledgeable than you, Umar."[13] In regards to the claims of Ali supposedly praising Umar's knowledge, Sunni and Shia agree that Umar said, "If it were not for Ali, Umar would have perished."[14]

From the viewpoint of other companions, "Umar b. al-Khattab took twelve years to learn *Surah al-Baqarah*, and when he learned it, he sacrificed a cow."[15] One of the transcribers of the Qur'an, Ubay b. Ka'ab said to Umar, "The reason for your lack of knowledge about the Qur'an is that the Qur'an was keeping me busy (with it), while you were busy in the marketplace."[16] Al-Bayhaqi says, "Since the house of Umar was far

---

[11] Ibn Abil Hadid, *Sharh Nahjul-Balaghah*, 1:61 and 1:182

[12] Ibid., 3:96

[13] *Tafseer al-Fakhr al-Raizi*, 3:175; *Tafseer al-Kashshaf*, 3:573; *Al-Jami li-Akham al-Qur'an*, 14:277; *Al-Durr al-Manthur*, 5:229

[14] Ibn Abd al-Birr, *Al-Estiaab*, 3:1103

[15] Ibn Asakir, *Al-Mukhtasar Tarikh b. Asakir*, 18:323

[16] Al-Bayhaqi, *Tafseer al-Qurtubi*, 7:69; 14:126

from the Mosque of the Prophet in the area of al-Awali, he used to go to the Mosque of the Prophet once every two days."[17]

Conversely, many unreliable hadith grossly exaggerate Umar's position and knowledge. One says, "If all of the knowledge of humanity was put on one side of a scale, and the knowledge of Umar was put on the other, then the knowledge of Umar would outweigh the knowledge belonging to all of humanity."[18] If this hadith was true, then what would be the need for the Prophet if Umar had all of this knowledge? Another "hadith" says, "One day an earthquake hit Madinah, and Umar hit the ground with his stick and said, 'Be calm, by the permission of Allah,' and the earthquake ceased because Umar told it to."[19] Moreover, another "hadith" claims that the Prophet said, "If I had never been sent to you as a prophet, Umar would have been sent by Allah as a prophet."[20] One hadith goes as far as to state, "In the nations before us, there were some people whom the angels would talk to, and if there is one person in our ummah that one is Umar."[21]

Although Umar looked to Ali for guidance during his caliphate, still Ali is purported to have said, "We used to say there is an angel speaking through the tongue of Umar."[22] While hadith pointing to the realistic good qualities of the second caliph would not be out of the ordinary; nonetheless, these traditions go beyond the bounds of credibility and suggest that Umar himself was higher than the Prophet was, and this is definitely an unacceptable belief.

Not all hadith regarding the second caliph came out of nowhere. Some hadith were specifically introduced to either counterbalance or share a similar tone in praising Ahlul Bayt or the immediate household of

---

[17] Ibid., 7:37

[18] *Al-Estiaab*, 2:430; Al-Hakim, *Al-Mustadrak*, 3:86

[19] *Tafseer al-Fakher al-Razi*, 21:88

[20] *Sunan al-Tirmidhi*, 5:281, hadith 3769; *Al-Mustadrak 'ala Sahihayn*, 3:85

[21] *Sahih al-Bukhari*, 5:15; *Sahih al-Muslim*, 4:1864/28; *Mustadrak 'ala Sahihayn*, 3:86

[22] Abu Nuaym, *Hiliyat al-Awliya*, 1:24

the Prophet. For example, Sunni and Shia both agree that the Prophet said about his daughter, "Fatima is part of me. Whoever angers her angers me, and whoever angers me angers Allah."[23] Therefore, the appearance of a similar hadith about Umar is not surprising - it reads, "Avoid angering Umar, for if he becomes angry, Allah will become angry."[24] Regarding one of the narrators of this hadith, Abu Luqman b. Asakir says, "He narrates false narrations and attributes them to people who are honest and trustworthy."[25]

Fortunately, many authentic hadith passed the test of time; nevertheless, numerous unfounded hadith remain. Moreover, such hadith continue to cause friction among the schools of thought. As an example, one fabrication that al-Dhahabi dismisses, in fact, he says, "This is a clear fabrication," is the hadith that reports:

> The first thing that Allah will embrace on the Day of Judgment is Umar b. al-Khattab, and the first thing that Allah will shake hands with is Umar b. al-Khattab, and the first who Allah will take his hand and go with him to Paradise is Umar b. al-Khattab.[26]

Another instance of a clearly erroneous hadith in the established books comes to us by Ibn al-Atheer who relates from Muhammad b. Khaleel, who al-Atheer himself said that he, Khaleel fabricates hadith[27] states:

> The Prophet climbed Mount Uhud with Abu Bakr, Umar, and Uthman. The mountain was shaking, so the Prophet kicked the mountain and

---

[23] *Al-Mustadrak ala Sahihayn*, 3:167, hadith 473; *Usd al-Ghabah*, 7:224; *Al-Isabah*, 4:378; *Al-Tahdheeb*, 12:469; *Majma al-Zawaid*, 9:203

[24] *Tarik Baghdad*, 3:49; Ibn Hajr, *Lisan al-Mizan*, 5:225

[25] Ibn al-Atheer, *Mukhtasar Tarikh b. Asakir*, 18:282

[26] Al-Dhahabi, *Al-Mizan*, 2:12

[27] Ibn al-Atheer, *Usd al-Ghabah*, 4:173

said, "Stop it Uhud, climbing you are only a prophet, a *siddiq* (truthful person), and two *shaheeds* (martyrs)."[28]

In *Sahih al-Muslim*, Ibn Abbas says:

> When Umar died and was lying on his bed, people were coming and praying for him. I felt a man holding my shoulders from my back. I saw that the man was Ali b. Abi Talib. He (Ali) began seeking forgiveness for Umar and said, "I wish I could meet Allah with the same deeds that Umar is meeting him with." Then he continued to say, "I hope that Allah will gather you (Umar) with your two companions (the Prophet and Abu Bakr) because I always heard the Prophet say, "I came with Abu Bakr and Umar; I left with Abu Bakr and Umar."[29]

Since Ali grew up side by side with the Prophet and spent virtually every moment with him, it is unlikely that the Prophet named others as being closer to him, especially since Umar himself narrated that the Prophet said, "Ali is the guardian (*mawla*) of every male and female believer."[30]

Attempting to prove that Umar was more insightful than the Prophet was someone related the following story:

> One day, Umar saw the Prophet ordering the Muslims to destroy the palm trees of Khaybar, so Umar asked the Prophet to stop doing that. The Prophet listened to Umar and asked the people not to cut down the palm trees of Khaybar.[31]

Unfortunately, this particular narration has been used to lower the status of the Prophet, whereas in fact, it is extremely unlikely that Allah

---

[28] Ibn Hajar, *Lisan al-Mizan*, 5:180

[29] *Sahih al-Muslim*, 4:1858, hadith 2389

[30] *Tafseer al-Tha'laby*, 4:92; Al-Thahabi Tarikh al-Islam, 3:633

[31] *Al-Sir al-Kabir*, 1:55

would send His final Messenger, perfect him in every way, and then leave him in need of basic guidance.

In another peculiar myth:

> When Egypt was conquered during the time of Umar b. al-Khattab, the people of Egypt came to the first governor, Amr b. al-Aas. They told him, "We have a tradition regarding the Nile River. On the eleventh of this month, we find a virgin woman and after seeking her parents' permission and satisfying them, we put the best clothing and ornaments on her, and then we throw her into the Nile. If we do not do this, then the river will not run." Amr b. al-Aas said, "No, this is against Islam, for this is injustice," and he banned them from this act. Since they did not throw a virgin woman into the Nile that year, it did not run and they had a drought so severe that they had to move (locations) due to a lack of water. When Amr b. al-Aas saw this, he wrote to Umar and asked him what to do. Umar wrote a letter to the river and asked his governor to throw the letter into the river. He wrote in the letter that he told the river, "If you are running by your own permission, then it is better that you do not run, but if you are running by the permission of Allah, then I ask that Allah make you run." They threw the letter into the river, and suddenly the river began running.[32]

While many fabrications focus on Umar, numerous others exist exaggerating the status of Abu Bakr and Uthman and sadly belittling the Holy Prophet. For example, in *Sahih al-Muslim*:

> The Prophet's thighs and legs were uncovered. Abu Bakr came, but the Prophet did not cover himself. Umar came, but he also did not cover himself. But when Uthman came, the Prophet sat and covered himself. When Lady Aishah asked him why he did that, the Prophet said,

---

[32] Al-Suyuti, *Tarikh al-Khulafa*, p. 127

"Should I not be modest in front of a man that the angels are shy in front of?"[33]

This narration is not in concordance with the high moral character of the Prophet. Seeing as the Prophet described Islam as a religion of modesty; it is difficult to imagine that he himself would be violating his own description of the path that he taught.

Similarly, in *Sahih al-Muslim* it says:

> One day, Lady Aishah was sitting next to the Prophet. Abu Bakr sought permission to enter while the Prophet was lying on his bed and Lady Aishah was sitting there. He came and the Prophet attended to Abu Bakr, and then Abu Bakr left. Then Umar came and the Prophet attended to him. Then Uthman came. When Uthman came, the Prophet told Lady Aishah, "Cover yourself." So she covered herself and the Prophet attended to Uthman. Then the Prophet turned to Lady Aishah and asked her, "Why were you not afraid when Umar and Abu Bakr came like you were when Uthman came?" She said, "Due to the fact that Uthman is a man with shame (*rajulun hayy*), and if I had remained (uncovered), then he would not have come and asked for what he needed, and I did not want to deprive him of obtaining what he required."[34]

Another story narrates that Allah sent the Angel Gabriel to ask Abu Bakr, "Are you happy with Allah? You are poor, do you accept this poverty?" Abu Bakr replied, "Should I be angry with Allah? No, I am happy with my God's decision. I am happy with my God's decision. I am happy with my God's decision." Al-Suyuti says regarding this hadith, "It is strange and the chain of narrators is weak."[35]

---

[33] *Sahih al-Muslim*, 4:1866, hadith 2401

[34] *Bab Fadahil Uthman*, 7:117, *Musnad Ahmad b. Hanbal*, 4:353; *Al-Adbe al-Mufrad, Sahih al-Buhkari*, p.131

[35] Al-Suyuti, *Tarikh al-Khulafa*, p.39

In another hadith it says, "Allah ordered the angels to penetrate the skies just like Abu Bakr is penetrating the earth." Regarding this claim, Ibn Kathir says, "This hadith is wrong and evil (*munkaran jiddan*)."

Al-Bukhari and Ahmad b. al-Hanbal relate that Lady Aishah said, "The Prophet was affected by magic by someone from Bani Zareeq named Lubayd b. al-Asal; and because of this spell, the Prophet would imagine that he had done something, but in fact he had not done it."[36]

Despite the poor performance of certain companions during the military excursions, fabrications about their bravery became abundant. When asked who was the bravest of the companions, Ali b. Abi Talib is said to have replied, "Abu Bakr - because on the day of Badr, we set up a tent for the Prophet, and we asked someone to stand next to him, so the *mushrikeen* (non-believers) would not attack him, none came forward except Abu Bakr. He raised his sword and stood there, thus he is the bravest person."

However, the Sunni historian, al-Tabari alludes to the unwillingness of Abu Bakr and Umar to fight, in addition to their frequent fleeing away from battles, such as in the Battle of Uhud and Hunain. Thus, the narrations that speak about their bravery are unjustifiable.[37]

Since Abu Bakr, Umar, Uthman, and Lady Aishah were the center of focus of such narrations, thus it may point to an element of untruth in them, since innumerable devoted companions, more than 100,000, aided the Prophet. Other books, such as *Kitab al-Maghazi* by al-Waqidi illustrates the same bias, mentioning Umar b. al-Khattab in 166 pages, and Abu Bakr in 143 pages, while he mentions only a few times other great companions such as Ammar b. Yasir, Musab b. Umair, Abdullah b. Masud, Khuzaymah b. Thabit, and Zayd b. al-Khattab (the brother of Umar).

---

[36] *Sahih al-Bukhari*, 7:28; *Musnad Ahmad b. Hanbal*, 6:57

[37] *Tarikh al-Tabari*, 2:240

Fabrications Involving the Qur'an

Some of the Umayyah clan went so far as to claim that some of the Qur'anic verses descended because of Umar's wishes, actions, and suggestions. For instance, al-Suyuti says:

> When Umar gave his opinion about something, the Qur'an would come with a verse supporting his opinion. Whenever there was a disagreement between the people and Umar, the Qur'an came and supported what Umar said... Allah supported Umar and confirmed his views in 21 places in the Qur'an.[38]

Such narrations claim that because Umar had instructed the Prophet not to seek forgiveness for the hypocrites that Allah revealed the following verse, "Whether you seek forgiveness for them or not, Allah will never forgive them." (c. 9:80) They also say that Umar suggested to the Muslims to prepare themselves for the Battle of Badr, and the Qur'an came in support of Umar's idea. However, these reports ironically neglect the fact that Umar is recorded to have been against the military engagement for the Battle of Badr. In addition, it is alleged that Allah revealed, "And whoever is the enemy of Allah and His angels and His Messengers and Gabriel and Michael, Lo! Allah is an enemy to those who reject faith," (c. 2:98) because Umar was defending the Angel Gabriel against a Jewish man who called the angel their enemy. Moreover, they maintain that the verse requiring people to seek permission before entering a person's chamber also came at the request of Umar.[39] These are all blatant tales trying to raise the status of Umar.

Imam al-Nawawi attributes many verses to Umar and says, "The Qur'an descended in conformance with Umar in many places, such as the prisoners of Badr, the verse of *hijab*, the station of Ibrahim, and the

---

[38] Al-Suyuti, *Tarikh al-Khulafa*, p.122-123

[39] Ibid., p.124

prohibition of wine."[40] However, the latter statement is extremely doubtful, since historians agree that Umar gradually ceased drinking.[41] In fact, the final verse prohibiting alcohol was revealed after Umar became drunk and injured the head of Abd al-Rahman b. Auf.

Hadith of the Twelve Successors

In addition to the fabrication of hadith, the ruling powers also took the trouble to change well-known traditions. One in particular reinforces their legitimacy and is a well-known hadith transmitted amongst both the Sunni and the Shia schools of thought.

Al-Bukhari, al-Muslim, Ahmad b. Hanbal, al-Tirmidhi, Abu Dawud, al-Tabarani, and Ibn Hajar all narrate the famous hadith which says, "The successors after me will be twelve, and all of them will be from Bani Hashim,"[42] except that in the *sahih* books, "Bani Hashim" has been changed to read "Quraysh."

How did the change in the hadith happen? According to al-Muslim, the narrator Jabir b. Samrah reports:

> I went with my father to see the Prophet and I heard him say that after him there would be twelve successors. Then he said something that I could not hear very well. I turned to my father and asked him, "What did the Prophet say?" My father said, "The Prophet said, 'All of them will be from Quraysh.'" [43]

Al-Bukhari relates the story somewhat differently, using the word "*amir*" (commander) instead of "*khalifah*":

---

[40] Al-Imam al-Nawawi, *Al-Tahdheeb*

[41] Al-Abshihi, *Al-Mustadraf*, 2:260; Ibn Shabbah, *Tarikh al-Madinah al-Muhawarah*, 3:863

[42] *Al-khulafa min badi ithna ashar wa kulluhum min Quraysh (Bani Hashim)*

[43] *Sahih al-Muslim*, 3:1452, hadith 5

I heard the Prophet say that there will be twelve *amirs*, but then said something I could not hear. I asked the person sitting next to me what the Prophet said and he replied, "All of them are from Quraysh."[44]

Abu Dawud says:

When the Prophet said, "There will be twelve successors after me," all the people began to do *takbir* (uttering "*Allahu akbar*") and raised their voices while the Prophet was speaking. Therefore, I could not hear the Prophet because all of the people were saying *takbir*. So I asked my father, "What did the Prophet say after that?" He said, "All of them will be from Quraysh."[45]

Ahmad b. Hanbal simply relates that Jabir b. Samrah says, "I heard the Prophet saying, 'This nation will have twelve successors,'[46] and 'all of them will be from Quraysh.'"[47] Al-Tabarani includes the same hadith, only using the word "*qayyim*" (guardian) instead of "*khalifah*."[48]

However, Ibn Hajar points to the root of the matter and explains that Jabir b. Samrah was sitting and could not hear the Prophet clearly. He turned to the two people next to him; one of them was his father and the other was Umar b. al-Khattab. As the Prophet was speaking, the people were listening quietly. Suddenly, when he approached the subject of who was to succeed him, clamor broke out (described in the other reports as *takbir*). Few could hear the Prophet clearly. However, according to Ibn Hajar, a person was ready to relate what the Prophet had said, and that was Umar b. al-Khattab - who as a key member of the

---

[44] *Sahih al-Bukhari*, 9:101

[45] *Sunan Abi Dawud*, 4:106, hadith 4280

[46] *Musnad Ahmad*, 5:106

[47] Ibid., 5:86

[48] Al-Tabarani, *Mujam al-Kabeer*, 2:196, hadith 1794

Quraysh group had a strong interest in ensuring that the caliphate was not limited to the members of Bani Hashim.[49]

In addition, Sunni scholars have had difficulty interpreting this hadith, since their number of successors to the Prophet never reached twelve. Shia scholars on the other hand, maintain that this hadith relates to the twelve Imams whom they say the Prophet designated to succeed him, one after another, beginning with Imam Ali b. Abi Talib and ending with Imam Muhammad al-Mahdi.

Where Did the Hadith Fictions Come From?

The fabrication of hadith flourished due to the initial ban on the transcription of the hadith that lasted for one century. Had Abu Bakr and Umar allowed the Muslims to write down the hadith, the Bani Umayyah would never have been able to attribute such lies to the Holy Prophet and his companions. Instead, the Bani Umayyah had free reign to encourage fabricators in their favor,[50] and in the words of Abu Jafar al-Iskafi:

> Mu'awiyah b. Abu Sufyan encouraged and paid some of the *sahabah* and the *tabieen* (the second generation of the *sahabah*) to fabricate evil hadith against Ali b. Abi Talib in order to slander, defame, vilify, and denounce him. He (Mu'awiyah) allocated an amount of money for them and they started inventing and creating these hadiths for him, which truly satisfied him. Among the fabricators were Abu Huraira, Amr b. al-Aas, al-Mugheerah b. Shu'bah, and Urwah b. Zubayr.[51]

A prominent Sunni historian adds:

---

[49] Ibn Hajar, *Fath al-Bari fi Sharh al-Bukhari*

[50] Mahmoud Abu Rayah, *Adwa ala al-Sunnah al-Muhammadiyah*, p.325

[51] Ibn Abil Hadid, *Sharh Nahjul-Balaghah*, 1:358

Mu'awiyah ordered all of his governors not to accept any testimony from the Shia of Ali (followers of Ali and the Ahlul Bayt). However, those who were the Shia of Uthman (the followers of Uthman and Bani Umayyah), were brought close, honored, paid, and their stories were documented until the virtues of Uthman were plenty and widespread. Then Mu'awiyah realized that there were too many hadith in favor of Uthman, so he said, "Go and from now on, say hadith in favor of the rest of the *sahabah* and the rest of the *khalifah* (Abu Bakr and Umar), and whenever you find a hadith narrated by the Prophet in favor of Ali, invent an identical one in favor of the *sahabah*. Remove from the public registry (*diwan*, list of salaries) whoever loves Ali and his family, and do not pay him his salary and destroy his house." [52]

As is apparent, the Bani Umayyah were ready and willing to contradict the Qur'an, known hadith, and even exaggerate the qualities and stature of Abu Bakr, Umar, and Uthman for the sake of political gain. Regrettably, they undermined the credibility of the hadith by fabricating a new Islam and turning its history inside out.

---

[52] Ibn Abd al-Birr, *Al-Istiab*, 1:65; Ibn Hajar, *Al-Isabah*, 1:154; Ibn Atheer, *Al-Kamil fil-Tarikh*, 3:162; *Tarikh al-Tabari*, 6:77

Chapter 9
Arduous Truth

﴿ ثُمَّ إِلَى رَبِّهِمْ مَرْجِعُهُمْ فَيُنَبِّئُهُمْ بِمَا كَانُوا يَعْمَلُونَ ﴾

In the end will they return to their Lord, and We shall then tell them the truth of all that they did.

Holy Qur'an, 6:108

Often Shias are asked by their Sunni counterparts, "Why do you hate the companions (*sahabahs*)?" The question resembles that which is asked by some of the Americans to the Muslims post 9-11, "Why do you (Muslims) hate us (Americans)?"

The truth is that the Shia do not hate the companions (*sahabahs*) of the Prophet; however, there are some of them who did not merit becoming the leaders of the ummah - and for rightful reasons. I ask the reader to bear with me as I present forth the research in this chapter, which will bring a better understanding as to why the Shia are not too fond of certain companions.

One of the primary beliefs in Sunni Islam is the sacredness of the sayings and deeds of the Holy Prophet's companions (the *sahabah*). Even today, merely inferring that a particular companion said or did something is enough to engender complete and total respect for that companion, and his words and deeds, and unquestioning compliance with what he or she said or did. For this reason, it is extremely important to investigate what exactly makes a person a *sahabah* of the Prophet. After all, thousands of people if not more, were in the presence of the Holy Prophet, and yet some of them were hypocrites and enemies of the Prophet according to the Qur'an;[1] therefore, how can they be relied upon?

Defining *Sahabah*

Al-Qaamus al-Muhit is the work of a prominent Sunni scholar and linguist; he defines *sahabah* as "*al-muasharah wa al-mulazimah*," which means living together or associating together inseparably. Raghib al-Isfahani says, "This term applies only to the one who is constantly and continuously in companionship (with another person)."[2] Therefore, according to these definitions, a companion of the Prophet would be someone who associated very closely with him, regardless of whether he was a Muslim or a non-Muslim, righteous or unrighteous, and whether he believed or disbelieved in him.

However, Islamic jurists (*usuliyun*) unanimously agree that for someone to bear the title of "companion," he or she must have been Muslim and must have accompanied the Prophet for a long period (*tallat mujalasatuhu*), while listening attentively to him and learning from him, not just merely visiting him or learning from or about his knowledge.[3]

The *Muhaddithun* (school of Narrators) defines "companion" as being "every Muslim who saw the Prophet."[4] Some scholars define it as, "any Muslim who lived during the time of the Prophet even if he did not see the Prophet."[5] Still other narrators further expanded the definition of

---

[1] "Round about you [Muhammad and his community] and among you in Madinah are hypocrites and they are obstinate in hypocrisy. You do not know them, We know them, twice shall We punish them and in addition they shall be sent to a grievous penalty." (9:101)

[2] *Al-Mufradat fi Gharib al-Qur'an*, the section on *Sahab*

[3] *Miqbaas al-Hidayah; Al-Darajat al-Rafia*, 10

[4] *Mukhtasar*, 2:67

[5] *Miqbaas al-Hidayah*

"companion" to encompass every Muslim who met the Prophet and believed in him, and then apostatized and then reverted to Islam.[6]

How the Sahabahs Define "Companionship"

In the earlier years of Islam, the Muslim ummah itself divided themselves into three categories in regards to how they viewed the *sahabah*:

(1) Al-Firqa al-Kamiliyah[7] and the Ghulat[8]

They were a minority sect of Muslims that attributed *kufr* (apostasy) to all of the companions. This view is of course, completely rejected by all modern scholars of Islam, in both the Sunni and Shia traditions.

(2) *Adalat al-Sahabah* – Integrity of the Companions

This group attributed absolute *adalah* (integrity) to all of the companions; this is the commonly held view within the Sunni tradition. For example, *Al-Khatib al-Baghdadi* says, "The justness of the *sahabah* is proven and firmly established (*thabitatun malumah*)."[9] Ibn Hazm says, "Undoubtedly, all of the companions are among the people of Paradise."[10]

Nevertheless, many prominent jurists and scholars in the Sunni tradition reject this idea of the absolute righteousness of all of the companions, and they include: al-Sa'd al-Tafatahzani, al-Marizi, and al-Shawqani,[11] as well as scholars from a later generation, such as Sheikh Muhammad Abduh, Sheikh Mahmud Abu Riyah, and others.[12] They

---

[6] Ibn Hajar al-Asqalani, 1:10

[7] The Kamilites – one of the schools of thought in Islamic theology.

[8] Those who attributed divinity to certain individuals.

[9] Ibn Hajar, *al-Isabah*, 1:17

[10] Ibn Hajar, *al-Isabah*, 1:19; Ibn Abd al-Birr, *al-Estiaab*, 1:8; Ibn al-Atheer, *Usd al-Ghabah*, 1:3

[11] Al-Sa'd al-Tafatahzani, *Sharh al-Maqasir*, 5:310; al-Marizi, *al-Isabah*, 1:19; al-Shawqani, *Irshad al-Fuhul*

[12] Sheikh Muhammad Abduh, *Adwa ala al-Sunnah Muhammadi*; Sheikh Mahmud Abu Riyah, *Abu Huraira*, 1:01

argued that the companions were not infallible, and thus there were the righteous and the unrighteous individuals amongst their ranks.

(3) The Qur'an, the Prophet, and the Ahlul Bayt

The Qur'an does not guarantee automatic righteousness to all of the Prophet's companions, nor does it grant all of them entrance into Paradise. Many of the righteous companions are praised and honored in the Qur'an, while others have been criticized - even cursed. The Qur'an says, "Round about you [Muhammad and his community] and among you in Madinah are hypocrites and they are obstinate in hypocrisy. You do not know them, We know them, twice shall We punish them and in addition they shall be sent to a grievous penalty." (c. 9:101) The Qur'an also says, "And Muhammad is not but an apostle, (other) apostles have already passed away prior to him; therefore, if he dies or is slain, will you turn upon your heels? And he who turns upon his heels will by no means do harm to God in the least, and soon will God reward the grateful ones." (c. 3:144) These and others verses, such as those found in *Surah al-Tawbah* (*Repentance*) and *Surah al-Munafiqun* (*The Hypocrites*) indicate that a group of hypocrites existed among the companions of the Prophet. Thus, according to the Qur'an, a group of companions was composed of the righteous and the unrighteous, the believers and the hypocrites, and although companionship was a great honor, it did not ensure immunity from error and this view has been adopted by the Shia scholars as well.

In many of the hadith, the companions themselves rejected each other or refuted what other companions said. As for the leaders of the Islamic schools of thought, Imam Abu Hanifah is known to have said that all of the companions were pure except for a few, and he mentioned some of their names.[13] Imam Malik b. Anas was asked what to do when two narrators relate contradictory hadith from the Prophet and whether both should be accepted or not? He replied that, no, the truth is only one; and when he was asked about the disagreement of the companions

---

[13] Ibn Abil Hadid, *Sharh Nahjul-Balaghah*

(*ikhtilaaf al-sahabah*), he said that one side is right and the other is wrong, and that the matter had to be investigated.[14] Imam al-Shaf'i states that he does not accept the testimony of four known companions: Mu'awiyah b. Abu Sufyan, Amr b. al-Aas, al-Mugheerah, and Ziyad.[15]

Hadith of "the Stars"

In the Sunni tradition, a famous hadith, known as the *Hadith of the Stars* reports that the Prophet said, "My companions are like the stars: whichever you follow, you will be guided."[16] Although this hadith is pivotal to the Sunni belief since it gives absolute certainty that all of the companions were entitled to lead others toward Paradise; nonetheless, Imam Ahmad b. al-Hanbal states that this hadith is unauthentic.[17] Abu Ibrahim al-Muzni, a student of al-Shaf'i, and his companions also doubted the authenticity of this hadith.[18] Abu Bakr al-Bazzaz criticized this hadith and expounded upon its flaws.[19]

Other narrators (*huffaz*) also mention its weakness and the unreliability of its chain of narrators. They include: Abul Hasan al-Darqutni, al-Bayhaqi, Ibn Hazm, Ibn Abd al-Birr, Ibn Asakir, Ibn al-Jawzi, Ibn Dahiyah, Abu Hayan al-Andalusi, Shams al-Din al-Dhahabi, and surprisingly, Ibn Qayyim al-Jawziyah.[20] In addition, Ibn Hajar al-Asqalani has stated that although famous, this hadith had an unreliable and weak chain of narrators (*isnad*).

Given these doubts, this hadith - one of the most important pillars of the concept of absolute righteousness of the companions - falls apart and is nothing more than a fabrication.

---

[14] Ibn Abd al-Birr, *Jami Bayan al-Ilm*

[15] Abul Fida, *al-Mukhtasar fi Akhbar al-Bashar*

[16] "*Ashabi kal-nujum...*"

[17] *Al-Taysir fi Sharh al-Tahrer*, 3:243, *Al-Muntakhab*, Ibn Qudamah

[18] Ibn Abd al-Birr, *Jami Bayan al-Ilm*, 2:89

[19] Ibn Abd al-Birr, *Jami Bayan al-Ilm*, 2:90; *Ilam al-Muwaqain*, 2:223; *Al-Bahr al-Muhit*, 5:528

[20] *Ilam al-Muwaqain*, 2:223

Flaws found in the Companions in the Established Hadith

The Prophet has been quoted as saying, "I am the first who will reach the fountain of *Hawdh al-Kawthar* (located in Paradise). Some people will try to reach me, but they will not be able to. I will say, 'O my Lord, they are my companions!' Allah will answer, 'You do not know what they have invented after you.'"[21]

This hadith reflects that some of the companions did indeed err. Anyone who considers them all to be just would be disregarding this hadith. If all of the companions were considered to be just, then one must question as to why some of the companions who murdered Uthman b. al-Affan will go to Heaven? To say because they were companions would not justify entrance into Heaven.

Even more, anyone who considers them all to be just must also ponder why some of them revolted against Ali - the rightful ruler who had proven his loyalty to Allah, the Prophet, and Islam, and had partaken in the civil battles of Jamal, Siffeen, and Nahrawan, in which thousands of Muslims lost their lives, so will these companions who fought against him also be rewarded with Paradise?

Participation of the Companions in the Battles

Despite popular misconception, neither Abu Bakr, Umar, nor Uthman participated actively in the main excursions of Islam. Not until the time of Mu'awiyah did the fabrications about their roles in these battles begin to surface in an effort by the Bani Umayyah to attribute the virtues of the Ahlul Bayt to others.

According to Ibn Arafah, "Most of the hadith which have been fabricated and developed in favor of the *sahabah*, their virtues, bravery, and heroism were fabricated during the time of the Bani Umayyah in

---

[21] *Sahih al-Bukhari; Sahih al-Muslim, Bab al-Hawdh*, 7:65; *Musnad Ahmad b. al-Hanbal*, 5:333

order to seek nearness to them, and to defy and humiliate the Bani Hashim."[22]

Battle of Uhud

On the day of the Battle of Uhud, the Holy Prophet raised his sword and called, "Who can give this sword its right?" Umar said, "I can," but the Prophet turned away from him, for he knew that Umar would not do that. Zubayr b. Awam said, "I can," but the Prophet refused him as well. Then Abu Dujanah stood and asked, "What is the right of that sword?" The Prophet replied, "You fight with it until it breaks." Abu Dujanah swore, "I am the one who will give it its right," so the Prophet gave his sword to Abu Dujanah.[23]

The Battle of Uhud commenced and in this regard, al-Tabari says:

> Ali b. Abi Talib began slaying the leaders of the battalions of the *mushrikeen* (people who associate others with God) in Uhud who were carrying the banners. Whenever a leader of another battalion would approach the Prophet, he (the Prophet) would look at Ali and say, "Start your strike on him," so he would strike them and disperse them. Group after group came and Ali b. Abi Talib did the same, until Gabriel came to the Prophet and said, "O Messenger of Allah, this is real solidarity." The Prophet said, "Yes, because he is part of me, and I am part of him." Gabriel replied, "And I am from both of you, O Messenger of Allah."[24]

What happened next in the Battle of Uhud has been recorded for eternity in the Holy Qur'an. Allah says, "Behold, you were climbing up the high ground, without even casting a side glance at anyone, and the Messenger in your rear was calling you back." (c. 3:153) This verse

---

[22] Ahmad Amin, *Fajr al-Islam*, p.213

[23] Al-Bayhaqi, *Dalail al-Nubuwah*, 3:218; Ibn Qutaybah, *Al-Marif*, p.159

[24] Al-Tabari, 2:197; Ibn al-Atheer, *Al-Kamil fil-Tarikh*, 2:154

indicates the opposition that the Holy Prophet had faced in maintaining his forces.

Examining the verse deeper and its *tafseer* (explanation), it explicitly identifies Abu Bakr, Umar, and the other companions - all of whom fled the scene except for a few who stood with the Holy Prophet – and this included one woman, Naseebah Umme Amarah b. Ka'ab (who fought until she was wounded on her shoulder), a few from the Ansar tribe, and Ali b. Abi Talib and Abu Dujanah from the Quraysh.[25] As Muhammad Hasanain Haykil says, "The main concern of every Muslim on that day was to rescue himself and salvage himself, except for those who had been protected and blessed by Allah, such as Ali b. Abi Talib."[26]

The Qur'an continues, "It was *Shaytan* (Satan) who caused them to fail because of some evil that they had done." (c. 3:153) Most likely, the "evil they had done" was their disobedience to the Holy Prophet, for although the Holy Prophet ordered them to remain in their positions, they ran after the war booty, thus the *mushrikeen* defeated them.

During his caliphate, Umar recalled that incident when his daughter and a woman came to him, asking for clothing. Umar gave some clothing to the woman but not to his daughter and when asked why he did that, he replied, "The father of that lady stood on the day of Uhud and did not run away, but the father of this one (pointing to his own daughter) ran away on the day of Uhud and did not stand firm."[27] Abu Bakr too later recounted his flight on that day.[28]

Although most of the companions returned a few hours after the Battle of Uhud, Uthman disappeared for three days.[29] When he returned,

---

[25] *Sahih al-Muslim* 5:78; *Dalail al-Nubuwah*; Al-Bayhaqi, 3:234; Al-Dhahabi, *Tarikh al-Islam*, p. 191

[26] Muhammad Hasanain al-Haykil, *Hayatu Muhammad*, p. 244

[27] Ibn Abil Hadid, *Sharh Nahjul-Balaghah*, 15:22

[28] al-Haykil, *Hayat Muhammad*, p.245

[29] *Mafatih al-Ghayb*, 9:53; *Tafseer al-Fakhr al-Razi*, 3:198; *Al-Serah al-Halabiyah*, 2:227

the Holy Prophet admonished him by saying, "It took you so long to return! Why three days?"[30]

Battle of Badr

A similar situation arose during the Battle of Badr. On the eve of the battle, Abu Bakr and Umar staunchly refused to fight. They said to the Holy Prophet, "This is Quraysh. The Quraysh are so powerful. The Quraysh never believed when they disbelieved. The Quraysh have never been defeated because they are so powerful, so do not fight them."

Displeased, the Prophet turned away from them, until Sa'd b. Ma'adh promised the Prophet, "Go and we will fight with you to the last breath." At that the Prophet became pleased again, and on the morning of the 17th in the month of Ramadhan (2 AH), the Muslims engaged against the *mushrikeen* in the Battle of Badr.[31] Seventy *mushrikeen* met their end in the battle, half of them exclusively by the sword of Ali, and the other half with the help of Ali's sword.[32]

Similarly, Uthman was not present during the Battle of Badr, just as he was not present at the important signing of Bay'at al-Ridhwan; what's more, he fled from the battles of Uhud and Hunayn. During the Battle of Khandaq, he refused to fight Amr b. Abd al-Wudd al-Aamir. Even after the death of the Prophet, he declined to participate in the battles against those who rejected the caliphate of Abu Bakr. During the time of Umar, he also refused to participate in any form of military service and was known for avoiding battles; his former ally, Abd al-Rahman b. Auf sarcastically chided him with this comment, "I was not the one who was absent from Badr, and I was not the one who ran away on the day of Uhud."[33]

---

[30] Ibn al-Atheer, *Al-Kamil fil-Tarikh*, 2:158; Ibn Katheer, *Al-Bidayah wal-Nihayah*, 4:32; *Tarikh al-Tabari*, 2:203

[31] Ibn Katheer, *Al-Serah al-Nabawiyah*, 2:391-395; *Dalail al-Nubuwah*, 3:106; *Al-Bidayah wal-Nihayah*, 3:321

[32] *Maghazi al-Waqidi*, 1:152; *Dalail al-Nubuwah*, 3:124

[33] Ibn Shabah, *Tarikh al-Madinah al-Munawarah*, 3:1033

Battle of Khaybar

The Battle of Khaybar took place during the seventh year of the migration, about 160 km north of Madinah. Due to the terrain, and the mighty fortress that the Jews barricaded themselves in, the first attempt to break through was led by Abu Bakr, who returned defeated. The second attempt, led by Umar, was also unsuccessful. Muslim historians have noted, "They returned not only defeated but exchanging blames of cowardice on each other."[34]

After the first two failed attempts, the Holy Prophet pledged, "Tomorrow, I will give this banner, the leadership of this battle, to a man who is loved by Allah and His Apostle, and he himself loves Allah and His Apostle. Allah will open the way by his hands. He will go forward and not be defeated or retreat." When the Prophet spoke these words, Ali was ill. Some of the companions brought him to the Prophet. As Ali leaned on the Holy Prophet, the Prophet prayed for him, placed the banner in his hands and said, "O Allah, may the heat and the cold not affect him anymore." Ali later stated, "After the prayer of the Prophet, I did not feel any heat or cold."[35] From there, Ali went and defeated Marhab, the Jewish leader of the enemies in the castle, including Marhab's two brothers, Harith and Yasir.[36]

Battle of Hunayn

The Prophet had brought 10,000 soldiers with him to recapture Mecca, and only a few days after their conquest of Mecca in the eighth year of the Hijrah, the Battle of Hunayn broke out. Two thousand more people in Mecca accepted Islam and joined the defense force. Therefore, the Prophet's army of 12,000 met their enemy in the valley of Hunayn between Mecca and the city of Taif.

---

[34] Al-Haythami, *Majma al-Zawaid*, 9:124; *Sahih al-Bukhari*, 4:465, hadith 1155; Muhammad Hasanain Hayqil, *Hayat Muhammad*, p.312

[35] Al-Dhahabi, *Tarikh al-Islam*, 2:412

[36] *Al-Sirah al-Halabiyah*, 3:39; *Maghazi al-Waqidi*, 2:654; *Sirat b. Hisham*, 3:349; *Tarikh al-Tabari*, 2:200

Like the Battle of Uhud, the Battle of Hunayn is mentioned in the Holy Qur'an, "Assuredly, Allah did help you in many battlefields, and on the day of Hunayn; behold, your great numbers elated you, but they availed you nothing; the land did constrain you, and you turned back fleeing." (c. 9:25-26) According to the *Tafseer* of this verse, seeing their large numbers, Abu Bakr exclaimed, "No one will defeat us while we have such a large number."[37] However, their numbers were meaningless since faith, bravery, sincerity, and willingness was lacking.

Although many companions pledged that they would not flee,[38] despite their vow, some still did leave including Abu Bakr, Umar, Uthman, Ibn al-Jarah, al-Mugheerah b. Shu'bah, Abu Musa al-Ashari, Ma'adh b. Jabal, Usayd b. Hubayr, Khalid b. al-Waleed, and Sa'd b. Abi al-Waqqas.[39] During the battle, Abu Sufyan, who had just become Muslim two weeks before, said about the Muslims, "I wish their defeat would not stop, and they would keep running away and fleeing until they reach the sea."[40] At the battle, only four stood with the Holy Prophet: Ali b. Abi Talib, al-Abbas - the uncle of the Prophet, Abu Sufyan b. al-Harith (from the Bani Hashim), and Abdullah b. Masud.[41] The rest of the companions fled the scene.

Conquests of the First Three Caliphs

Along with his army, the Messenger of Allah always fought on the frontlines of the battle; but such was not the case for Abu Bakr, Umar, and Uthman - they never battled alongside their soldiers during their years as caliphs. Instead, they sat in Madinah and dispatched forces.

---

[37] Al-Zamakhshari, *Tafseer al-Kashshaf*, 2:259; *Tarikh Abul Fida*, 1:208; *Al-Serah al-Halabiyyah*, 3:110

[38] *Sunan al-Nisai*, 3:871, hadith 3877

[39] *Maghazi al-Waqidi*, 2:904

[40] *Maghazi al-Waqidi*, 2:904

[41] *Tarikh al-Khamis*, p.102; *Al-Serah al-Halabiyah*, 3:109

When Abu Bakr assumed the caliphate, rather than fight himself, he sent Usama b. Zayd to fight the Romans. When Usama inquired as to why Umar was remaining in Madinah, Abu Bakr said that he needed him there. When Usama then asked Abu Bakr why he himself was staying behind in Madinah, Abu Bakr told him, "Just lead the army and go."[42]

When the Bani Umayyah came to power, they fabricated stories saying that Ali advised Umar and Abu Bakr not to lead their armies, since they were the leaders of the people. Such stories are obviously false, since during his own caliphate, Ali himself led his troops and thus he would not have advised others to do contrary to this.

Despite the unwillingness of the first three caliphs to participate in military activity, the Muslim conquest during their caliphate was tremendous. The Islamic influence spread far and during the reign of Umar, the Persian and Roman Empires were both defeated. However, the motive of the first three caliphs to send the Muslims into battle was less for military necessity than it was to prevent political unrest at home. This ploy is most visible in the advice that Abdullah b. Aamir gave to Uthman b. al-Affan when he instructed him to keep the Muslims preoccupied in battle so that Uthman would have less difficulties with the masses.

A Brief Introduction to the Prophet's Companions

Abu Bakr (b. Abi Quhafah)

The Holy Prophet gave Abu Bakr the surname of Abdullah.[43] Before that, he was known as *Abd al-Ka'abah* (the worshipper of the Ka'abah) and *al-Ateeq* (the freed one). Although Lady Aishah had been quoted as stating that the Prophet called Abu Bakr, *Ateeq Allah min al-Nar* (the person whom Allah has vindicated from the Fire);[44] however, sources indicate

---

[42] *Tarikh al-Tabari*, 2:462

[43] Ibn Qutaybah, *Al-Marif*, 167

[44] *Tarikh al-Tabari*, 2:615

that Abu Bakr's father had called him *Ateeq* long before Islam because of the delicacy of his skin.[45] His mother's name is reported as being Salma b. Sakher.

Abu Bakr was the fifteenth man to embrace Islam,[46] not the first, as some may believe and in his early days, he made a living selling clothing, as did Uthman b. al-Affan, Abd al-Rahman b. Auf, and Talha b. Ubaydillah.

Umar b. al-Khattab b. Nafeel b. Uday b. Ka'ab[47]

Umar b. al-Khattab was born thirteen years after the Year of the Elephant, thus he was thirteen years younger than the Prophet was, eleven years younger than Abu Bakr, and seven years younger than Uthman b. al-Affan. While still young, his mother was adopted by Hisham b. al-Mugheerah, so she was known as Hantamah b. Hisham b. al-Mugheerah.[48] He made a living as a merchant dealer and died at the age of eighty-six in the year 23 AH.

At the age of forty-six, he became a Muslim and was the seventy-fifth person to accept Islam. He did so right before the migration from Mecca to Madinah; thus, he did not participate in the first Hijrah to Ethiopia.[49]

Before joining the Muslims, Umar exhibited an enormous dissatisfaction towards Islam and the Muslims so much so that he beat his brother-in-law and hit his sister when he discovered that they had become Muslims.[50] Perhaps for this reason, Umar had been chosen by the rest of the Quraysh to kill the Prophet.[51]

---

[45] *Tabaqat b. Sa'ad*, 3:187

[46] *Tarikh al-Tabari*, 2:316

[47] *Tarikh al-Madinah al-Munawarah*, 2:654

[48] Ibn al-Atheer, *Usd al-Ghabah*, 4:145

[49] *Tarikh al-Tabari*, 5:17

[50] Al-Aqad, *Abqariyat Umar*, p. 33

[51] Ibn Ishaq, *Al-Serah al-Nabawiyah*, 160; Ibn Asakir, *Mukhtasar Tarikh Damashq*, 18:271

It is mentioned that one day, Umar took his sword and went to the house of Ibn Abi al-Arqam, where the Holy Prophet was with his uncle, Hamzah and some companions. He knocked loudly and burst into the house angrily. The Prophet restrained him and shook him so hard that he fell to the ground. The Prophet then said, "Isn't it time that you stop your persecution and terrorization of the Muslims?" At which Umar replied, "I bear witness that there is no God but Allah, One with no partner, and I bear witness that Muhammad is His servant and messenger."[52]

Throughout his life, Umar was known for his violent nature and outbursts. He usually frowned at people and often used his hand to strike the Muslims, and during his caliphate, he was often seen using his stick (*durrah*), to strike people. He quickly angered and judged others with the same rapidity.

He was known to be particularly harsh with women, whether they were his daughters, his wives, his sisters, or strangers. He once wrote, "I buried my daughter alive, and while I was burying her, she was putting her hands on my beard to clean the dust from it."[53] Al-Ashath b. Qays recalls that when he was hosting Umar at his home, in the middle of the night, Umar kept beating his wife until al-Ashath stopped him.[54] Umar told another one of his wives, "You are nothing but a toy that men play with, and then you are abandoned."[55] His harshness caused women to decline his marriage proposals; one of those who refused him was Umme Kulthum, the daughter of Abu Bakr.[56]

Umar did not confine his abuse to only the women of his household. When Lady Aishah was mourning the death of her father Abu Bakr, he threatened to hit her if she did not stop and then retorted to beating her

---

[52] Ibn Asakir, *Mukhtasar Tarikh Damashq*, 18:269

[53] Al-Aqad, *Abqariyat Umar*, p. 33

[54] *Sunan b. Majah*, 1:693, *Musnad Ahmad*, 1:20

[55] Ibn al-Jawzi, *Tarikh Umar b. al-Khattab*, p.114; *al-Shaykhan*, p.189

[56] Al-Tabari, *Tarikh al-Umam wal-Muluk*, 5:17; Ibn Atheer, *al-Kamil fil-Tarikh*, 3:54

sister, Umme Farwah with his stick instead. Hence, they both stopped crying.[57] On another occasion, when he heard the cry of a woman, he took it upon himself to enter her home and hit her with his stick, until the covering of her hair fell off.[58] When Zaynab, the Prophet's daughter died, Umar hit the women who were crying over her, until the Messenger of Allah seized his hand and told him to stop.[59] Needless to say, even Fatima al-Zahra, the daughter of the Holy Prophet did not escape his wrath. Tragically, Umar attacked her at her own home and forced her to miscarry her baby son Muhsin, the third grandson of the Holy Prophet.

Numerous traditions relate that the Muslim community greatly feared Umar's violent tendencies. However in one tradition, although unbecoming, it shows the extent of that fear. In an example of the virtues of Umar b. al-Khattab, al-Bukhari relates a peculiar story:

> Some women were sitting with the Prophet and enthusiastically asking him questions that caused their voices to be raised above the voice of the Prophet. Umar sought permission to enter, and as soon as the women heard him, they became afraid and put on their *hijab* (head covering). After the Prophet gave him permission, he entered, at which point the Prophet laughed. Umar asked the Prophet, "Why do you laugh, O Messenger of Allah?" The Prophet replied, "I am surprised at these women who were sitting next to me not wearing the *hijab*, but the moment they heard your voice, they rushed to wear the *hijab*." Umar rebuked them, "You are the enemies of Allah; why do you not fear the Prophet and you fear me?" They told him, "Due to the fact that you are harsh and violent."[60]

---

[57] Ibn Hajir, *al-Isabah*, 3:606; Ibn Sa'd, *Tabaqat b. Sa'd*, 3:208

[58] Ibn Abil Hadid, *Sharh Nahjul-Balaghah*, 3:111

[59] *Musnad Ahmad b. Hanbal*, 1:237; *Mustadrak al-Hakim*, 3:191

[60] *Bab al-Tabasum*, 4:63

Al-Bukhari considers this narration to be an example of the virtues of Umar b. al-Khattab - perhaps it may be that this tradition reflects the fear of Umar amongst the women; but it also implies that the Prophet was frolicking amongst unveiled Muslim women, and such an implication undermines the moral virtues and character of the Prophet.

In another incident, Umar summoned a woman whose chastity he doubted so that he could inquire whether her pregnancy was legitimate. Terrified, the woman miscarried. When Umar asked his aides whether he had to pay the *diyah* (blood money), they told him that he did not have to because he was only instructing her. However, Ali instructed him, "They misled you, they ill-advised you and you have to pay the *diyah* of the baby to its mother."

Men too were on the receiving end of Umar's *durrah* (stick). People used to say, "The stick of Umar is sharper than the sword of al-Hajjaj (al-Hajjaj was a well-known tyrant who had killed thousands of his opponents)."[61] Ibn Sa'dah al-Hadhalah narrates, "I saw Umar b. al-Khattab in the market beating the merchants with his stick. When they gathered around the food in the market, he wanted to disturb them, so he used his stick."[62] When he was not using his stick, he often used his hands or his feet, and sometimes he would bite people. In one instance, he bit the hand of Ubaydallah b. Umar, the son of a man who was known as Abu Isa, and warned him, "Do not call yourself Abu Isa, since Isa [Prophet Jesus] did not have a father."[63]

Again in the market, he beat people for purchasing red meat, which was considered a delicacy, two days in a row.[64] In addition, he beat Timem al-Darimi for performing the *sunnah* (recommended) prayers after the afternoon prayers.[65] He even beat the man who later became a

---

[61] *Tarikh al-Madinah Al-Munawarah*, 2:686

[62] *Tabaqat b. Sa'd*, 5:60

[63] *Umdat al-Qari*, 7:143

[64] Al-Haythami, *Majma al-Zawaid*, 5:35

[65] Al-Haythami, *Majma al-Zawaid; Sahih al-Muslim*, 1:310; *Musnad Ahmad b. Hanbal*, 4:102

popular transmitter of hadith, Abu Huraira. Many other incidents of Umar's brutality have been reported by the companions, such as Bilal[66] and Abd al-Rahman b. Auf.[67] Even Umar himself knew he was too harsh and once prayed, "O my Lord, I am tough, so make me soft."[68]

Unlike his predecessor Abu Bakr, Umar was known for his toughness, even sometimes, he was merciless.[69] Umar's toughness caused many of the companions in Madinah to react against him. Openly, the Muslims could not retaliate against him, thus the people would aim their stones at him during the stoning of the symbolic *Shaytan* at the Hajj and cause him to bleed.[70]

In addition to using aggression, Umar b. al-Khattab also imprisoned many people during his caliphate. Al-Dhahabi relates that Umar detained three prominent companions: Abdullah b. Masud, Abu Dardah, and Abu Masud al-Ansari.[71] According to Abu Bakr b. al-Arabi, they were only released after Umar died.[72] Umar imprisoned these three because he feared they would spread certain hadith from the Prophet that threatened his rule.

Umar saw little value in the blood relationships between people and the Holy Prophet. When Safiyah, the aunt of the Prophet, whom the Prophet respected considerably lost her son, the Prophet consoled her by saying that Allah would build a house in Paradise for anyone who lost a child and was patient through the ordeal. After hearing this, Safiyah was comforted and the Prophet left her. Afterwards, Umar came and said to her, "Safiyah, I heard your cries, and your relationship to the Prophet will

---

[66] Al-Suyuti, *Tarikh al-Khulafa*, p.130

[67] Ibn Abil Hadid, *Sharh Nahjul-Balaghah*, 1:55

[68] *Tarikh al-Khamis*, 2:241

[69] *Tabaqat b. Sa'd*, 5:60; *Umdat al-Qari*, 7:143; *Sahih al-Muslim*, 1:310; *Musnad Ahmad*, 4:102; Ibn al-Jawzi, *Sirat Umar b. al-Khattab*, p.174; *Kanz al-Umal*, 4:334

[70] *Tabaqat b. Sa'd*, 5:64

[71] Al-Dhahabi, *Tadhkirat al-Huffaz*, 1:2; *Adwa ala Sunan Muhammadiyah*, p.45

[72] Abu Bakr b. al-Arabi, *Al-Awasim min al-Qawasim*, p.75-76

not help you on the Day of Judgment." At that, she started crying again. The Prophet heard her cry again and said, "O my aunt, you are still crying and you heard what I said to you?" She replied, "No, O Messenger of Allah, what made me cry again was when Umar said to me that my relationship to the Prophet would not help me on the Day of Judgment." Angered, the Prophet told Bilal to call for the prayer (*adhan*), and when the people assembled, he climbed the pulpit, praised Allah and asked, "What is wrong with the people that they claim that my relationship does not benefit them and is useless on the Day of Judgment? My relationship is binding in this world and in the Hereafter."[73]

Umar is also recorded to have had a propensity towards music and wine (*nabeeth*[74]).[75] He habitually listened to and requested music to be played and he is said to have stayed awake until dawn to listen to singing (*ghina*).[76]

Since wine was initially discouraged rather than prohibited, some Muslims continued to drink between the Qur'anic revelations of c. 2:219 and c. 4:42 and Umar was one of those who drank between the revelations. Once while drunk, he fractured the head of Abd al-Rahman b. Auf and then sat poetically lamenting the *mushrikeen* who had been killed in the Battle of Badr. At that moment, Allah revealed the third verse that completely prohibited the drinking of alcohol (wine).[77] Having realized Allah's commandment that there was no more permissibility for drinking, Umar cried out, "We stopped (*intahayna*), we stopped (*intahayna*)."[78] However, during his caliphate, Umar is recorded to have continued to ask for wine - once when he was traveling to Shaam

---

[73] Al-Haythami, Majm al-Zawaid, 8:216

[74] *Nabeeth* is a form of wine.

[75] Al-Aqad, *Abqariyat Umar*, 61:265

[76] *Sunan al-Kubra al-Bayhaqi*, 5:69; *Al-Muhalla*, 9:62; *Al Tabaqaat al-Kubraa*, 4:163

[76] *Holy Qur'an*, 5:91; Ibn Sa'd, *Al Tabaqaat al-Kubraa*, 4:163

[77] *Holy Qur'an*, 5:91

[78] "*Intahayna, intahayna*;" *Al-Mustadraf*, 2:499-500; *Jami al-Bayan*, 2:211

(Syria);[79] and once when he was traveling to Mecca, he met a man named Abdullah b. Ayash al-Maszumi and sipped his wine before passing it on to the man on his right.[80] Other stories have also been recorded; however, the last known incident of him drinking alcohol was after doing his prayers just before he was killed.[81] However, some tend to explain these stories by saying that the wine that Umar drank after the time of *jahilliyah* was non-alcoholic.

Qur'an as a "Book"

By the time Umar became the caliph, Muslims already had the Qur'an in its complete and present-day form. Many verses of the Qur'an also attest to its preserved status before the life of the Prophet ended.[82] The Prophet handpicked the scribes who would copy word for word each *ayah* (considered as a letter or a word in the Qur'an) under his direct supervision. The known scribes were: Ali b. Abi Talib, Abdullah b. Masud, Abu Dardah, Zayd b. Thabit, Ma'adh b. Jabal, and Salim Mawla Abi Hudayfah. During the lifetime of the Prophet, many of the companions - forty-one of whom are recorded by Ibn Nadeem[83] - had written the entire Qur'an with their own hands; therefore, each copy was known as "the copy of Abdullah b. Masud," "the copy of Ibn Abbas," and so on.

In later times, some attempted to credit Abu Bakr and Umar for first compiling the Qur'an, but those who did so neglected the earlier historical references. In reality, Umar not only lacked interest in the Qur'an, but he also cast serious doubt on its completeness and authenticity. Oftentimes, he would inform the people from the *minbar* (pulpit) that some verses of the Qur'an were removed.

---

[79] *Tabaqat Ibn Sa'd*, 3:230

[80] *Muwatta Imam al-Malik*, 2:894

[81] *Sahih al-Bukhari; Tabaqat b. Sa'd*, 3:257; *Istiab of Ibn Abd al-Birr*, 3:1154

[82] *Holy Qur'an*, 80:13-15, 76:77-79, 25:5, & 98:2

[83] Ibn Nadeem, *Al-Fihrist*, p. 41

Even more, Umar believed that certain verses were lost with the death of the Prophet.[84] In accordance with al-Bukhari, Umar is related to have said, "Allah sent Muhammad with the truth, and He sent a book to him, and we used to read verses in that book, and we don't find them anymore." The "missing" verse that Umar is referring to - in which only he thought - was about stoning of an adulterer.[85]

At times, during the dawn prayers, Umar would recite verses that no one else heard; he called them "*al-hafd wal-khul.*"[86] As for the entirety of the Qur'an, Umar mentioned that it was composed of a whopping 1,027,000 letters, while the Qur'an consists of just over 300,000 letters.[87]

Umar would argue, for instance, with one of the original transcribers of the Qur'an, Hudayfah. Umar asked him how many verses were in *Surah al-Ahzab*, and Hudayfah answered that there were 72 or 73. Umar countered that the number of verses in that *surah* was similar to the number of verses in *Surah al-Baqarah*, which has 286 verses, implying that over 200 verses of the original *surah* had been lost.[88] He also said that *Surah al-Tawbah* (*Repentance*) was only one-fourth of the original, and that it was first called "Surah al-Adhab (The Punishment)" before the people changed its name to *Surah al-Tawbah*.[89]

Tafseer, the interpretation of the verses of the Holy Qur'an was also not one of Umar's strong points. He would often discourage, even react violently when people asked him questions about the meaning of the Qur'an, which he could not answer.[90] When a man came to Umar and inquired about what c. 4:128 meant, Umar hit him rather than admitting

---

[84] Al-Suyuti, *Al-Durr al-Manthur*, 5:179

[85] *Sahih al-Bukhari*, 10:43; Abu Ubaydah, *Al-Itqan*, 2:42; Al-Suyuti, *Al-Dur al-Manthur*, 1:106

[86] Al-Suyuti, *Al-Dur al-Manthur*, 3:296; Al-Mutaqi al-Hindi, *Kanz al-Ummal*, 8:74-75 & 78

[87] Al-Suyuti, *Al-Dur al-Manthur*, 6:222; Al-Haythami, *Majma al-Zawaid*, 7:163; *Kanz al-Umal*, 1:517

[88] *Musnad Ahmad*, 5:132; *Mustadrak al-Hakim*, 2:415; *Sunan al-Bayhaqi*, 8:211

[89] *Mustadrak al-Hakim*, 2:330; Al-Suyuti, *Al-Durr al-Manthur*, 1:105

[90] Al-Muttaqi al-Hindi, *Kanz al-Ummal*, 1:229; Al-Suyuti, *Al-Durr al-Manthur*, 6:321

that he did not know the answer. Similarly, when someone asked Umar what "fodder" meant in the verse, "We split the earth in fragments and produce therein grain...and fruits and fodder"[91] Umar reproached him saying, "You have the book of your Lord with you. Practice what you know from it, and leave what you do not know."[92] According to Ibn Abil Hadid, Umar was not concerned with the interpretation (*tafseer*) of the Qur'an and used to say, "Just recite the Qur'an and do not interpret it (*tufassiruhu*),"[93] since he himself did not know much about it.

Occasionally, Umar would hear verses of the Qur'an but not recognize them as such.[94] One day, Umar angrily interrupted a man who was reading verse 11 from *Surah al-Tawbah* because he did not recognize the verse and assumed that the man was inventing it. Defending himself, the man asserted, "Yes, I heard it from Ubay b. Ka'ab," one of the transcribers of the Qur'an. Then, Umar went to Ubay b. Ka'ab and asked him three times about the verse. Each time he replied, "Yes, I received it from Prophet Muhammad." After that, Umar left raising his hands and shouting "*Allahu akbar* (God is Great)," "*Allahu akbar*," confessing that the verse was authentic but that he had never heard it before.[95]

Elsewhere, when Umar saw verse nine of *Surah al-Jumuah* (c. 62) written on a tablet he questioned, "Who dictated this verse to you?" Someone replied that Ubay b. Ka'ab had narrated the verse. Umar said, "The Prophet has died and we did not read this verse the way it is written here." He then continued that the verse should have read "*fa umdhu ilaa dhikr Allah*," instead of "*fasaw ilaa dhikr Allah*" (with both versions having the same meaning of "march" or "go").[96]

---

[91] *Holy Qur'an*, 80:31

[92] Al-Suyuti, *Al-Durr al-Manthur*, 6:317; Al-Muttaqi al-Hindi, *Kanz al-Ummal*, 2:328

[93] Ibn Abil Hadid, 3:2 &120

[94] Al-Muttaqi al-Hindi, *Kanz al-Ummal*, 2:568

[95] Al-Muttaqi al-Hindi, *Kanz al-Ummal*, 2:605

[96] *Sahih al-Bukhari*, 3:201

Umar himself knew that his knowledge of the Qur'an was lacking because once when he heard a man read verse 107 of *Surah al-Maidah*, he told him, "You are a liar." The man rebuked, "You are a liar." Another man interjected, "Are you denying that the Commander of the Faithful is saying the truth?" The man replied, "No, I respect the Commander of the Faithful, but he is unaware of the Qur'an." Umar admitted, "He is telling the truth (*sadaq*)."[97]

One of the scribers of the Qur'an, Ubay b. Ka'ab commented, "I was busy with the Qur'an during the time of the Prophet, but you (Umar) were busy walking in the markets and in the streets."[98]

An assailant stabbed Umar b. al-Khattab on Wednesday, four days before the end of Dhul Hijjah in 23 AH.[99] As his condition worsened he realized that his life was about to end, thus he began addressing the subject of his impending death with apprehension and anxiety. Abdullah b. Amar b. Rabiah relates:

> I saw Umar when he was on his deathbed, holding in his hand a piece of straw. He raised it and said, "I wish I was this straw. I wish I was nothing. I wish my mother had not delivered me."[100]

Soon after, he said:

> I wish I was a male sheep in my family. They would feed me and fatten me, and once I became fat, someone who likes my family would visit, so they would slaughter me. They would grill part of me and dry the

---

[97] Ibn Shabbah, *Tarikh al-Madinah al-Munawwarah*, 2:709

[98] Al-Muttaqi al-Hindi, *Kanz al-Ummal*

[99] Ibn al-Atheer, *Usd al-Ghabah*

[100] Al-Suyuti, *Tarikh al-Khulafa*, 129

second half. After that, they would eat me and turn me into *adharah* (human waste - feces). I wish I was not a human being. [101]

He expressed a similar sentiment again:

> I wish I was a tree on the side of a road, and a camel would pass by and eat me, and start to chew me and swallow me, and then get rid of me as its droppings. I wish I was not a human being. [102]

These statements raise many questions. Perhaps Umar was regretting how he had treated the Prophet, or how he had accused the Prophet of hallucinating,[103] or how he had delayed the burial of the Prophet until Abu Bakr had returned to participate in the power-sharing talks.[104] Perhaps he regretted tugging on the clothes of the Prophet while he was reading *Salat al-Janazah* (Prayer of the Deceased);[105] or raising his voice above the voice of the Prophet despite the command of the Qur'an to the contrary (c. 49:2). Maybe at the time of his death, the incident of the attack on the house of Fatima al-Zahra came to his mind.

Just before he died, Umar was resting his head in the lap of his son Abdullah. He asked his son to put his cheek on the ground. His son did not listen, so Umar repeated his words harshly. As soon as his cheek touched the earth, Umar said, "Woe to Umar and to the mother of Umar, if Allah does not forgive Umar." After the fatal attack on him on Wednesday, Umar was buried the following Sunday, the first day of Muharram, in 24 AH. His *khalifah* lasted for ten years, five months, and twenty-one days.

---

[101] Al-Suyuti, *Tarikh al-Khulafa*, 142; *Muntakhab Kanz al-Ummal*, 4:361, 6:365

[102] *Muntakhab Kanz al-Ummal*, 4:361

[103] *Sahih al-Bukhari*, 1.120; *Kitab al-Ilm*; *Sahih al-Muslim*, 11:89

[104] *Tarikh al-Tabari*, 2:442; *Sirat b. Hisham*, 4:305

[105] *Sahih al-Bukhari*; *Kitab al-Libas*; *Kanz al-Umaal*, hadith 4403

Uthman b. al-Affan

As mentioned elsewhere, the primary reason why Uthman was killed was for mismanaging the affairs of the Muslim nation, and it was Lady Aishah who was the forerunner to censure him regarding this.

While both the Prophet and Abu Bakr had distributed the revenue from the treasury equally amongst the Muslims, Umar, on the other hand, begun to shift the distribution in favor of his allies. Thus Umar had assigned Lady Aishah, the daughter of Abu Bakr; Hafsa, his own daughter; and Umme Habiba, the daughter of Abu Sufyan with 12,000 *dinars* a month, while providing the rest of the wives of the Prophet with only 5,000 *dinars* per month.

When Uthman came to power, he wanted to reinstate the equal stipend among the Prophet's widows but Lady Aishah protested,[106] and thus the campaign to turn against Uthman first began by her. According to al-Tabari,[107] she is recorded to have said, "Kill this Nathal[108] (the nickname she gave to Uthman), for he has disbelieved."[109]

Besides his practice of nepotism and favoritism, Uthman on many levels suspended the practices of the Qur'an and the Holy Prophet. Blatantly disregarding the two most fundamental aspects of Islam had undoubtedly caused a furor amongst the Muslim population, as a result of his actions, Uthman was murdered and his corpse was prohibited from being buried inside the Muslim cemetery of al-Baqi,[110] and to add to this, the prayer of the deceased was prohibited from being performed on him.[111]

---

[106] *Tarikh al-Yaqubi*, 2:132

[107] Al-Tabari, 5:72

[108] Nathal was a Jewish man with a long beard who resided in Madinah at the time.

[109] *Tarikh al-Tabari*, 3:477; Ibn A'atham, *Al-Futuh*, 1:64

[110] When Mu'awiyah came into power, he extended the boundaries of al-Baqi cemetery to include the burial site of Uthman.

[111] *Tarikh al-Madinah al-Munawarah*, 3:1052

Further information about these individuals can be found in the history of al-Tabari.[112]

Innovations of Umar b. al-Khattab

According to historical records, Umar b. al-Khattab prided himself on his "improvements" to the teachings of the Qur'an and the Prophet. Although Abu Bakr and Uthman both adjusted religious law for special cases,[113] Umar relied almost entirely on his own opinion and encouraged others to do the same.

When he appointed Shurayh al-Qadi as the religious judge of Madinah, he instructed him, "If you are searching for a verdict, then look in the Book of God. If you do not find one, then look in the tradition of the Prophet. But if you do not find it in the tradition of the Prophet, then make up a verdict yourself."[114]

Similarly, he wrote to Abu Musa al-Ashari, "If you do not find an answer in the Book or the tradition, then make an analogy and develop an answer yourself."[115] For these reasons, al-Tabari says that people preferred not to take their disputes to Umar, because he was known for judging by his personal beliefs, rather than the Islamic criteria.[116]

---

[112] *Tarikh al-Tabari*, 2:452

[113] For example, Abu Bakr was unwilling to prosecute Khalid b. al-Waleed, who killed Malik b. Nuwayrah, and who on the same night, had committed adultery with the wife of the victim. Abu Bakr said, "He made *ijtihad* (deducing Muslim law), but of course he made an error," and left the matter at that.

[114] Muhammad al-Khudari, *Tarikh al-Tashri al-Islami*, p.83

[115] Ibid

[116] Al-Tabari, 2:617

Changes During Umar's Reign

Some of the practices that Umar is best known for changing are the *adhan* (call to prayer), *tarawih*[117] prayer, prayers for the deceased, and the laws of divorce which we will explain in detail:

Adhan (Call to Prayer)

Initially, "*as-salatu khayrun min an-nawm* (prayer is better than sleep)" was not part of the *adhan*. It came about one morning when Umar's servant came to wake him for prayer by calling to him, "*as-salatu khayrun min an-nawm*." Approving of that phrase, Umar instructed the *muadhdhin* (a person who performs the call to prayer) to include it in the *adhan* from then on.[118]

History of the Adhan

A majority of the Sunni commentators maintain that the Prophet learned the *adhan* from a companion named Abdullah b. Zayd. Narrators such as al-Tirmidhi, Abu Dawud, and Ibn Majah say that the Prophet asked his companions how he should inform people about the time for prayer. Some said he should use a banner, others said a horn, and others said a bell, like the Christians. According to these narrators, it is reported that on that night, Abdullah b. Zayd had the following strange dream:

> Abdullah b. Zayd saw a man carrying a bell in his hand. He asked if he could buy the bell, and the man asked him what he wanted it for. Abdullah b. Zayd said, "I want to use it to call the people to prayer." The man replied, "I can teach you something better than ringing the bell," and then he taught Abdullah b. Zayd the *adhan*.

---

[117] In the Sunni tradition, *tarawih* is done as a congregational prayer during the nights of the Month of Ramadhan, while the Shia perform it individually.

[118] Jalal al-Deen al-Suyuti, footnoted in *Tanweer al-Hawalik*, referencing *Muwatta Malik*; *Sunan al-Tirmidhi*, 1:64

According to these commentators, in the morning Abdullah b. Zayd told the Prophet his dream. The Prophet replied, "This is a true dream that you have seen. Come with me to Bilal - teach him what you have seen in the dream and let Bilal learn the *adhan*." The story concludes that when Umar heard the *adhan*, he told the Prophet, "I swear, I saw the same dream," and the Prophet said, "praise be to Allah."

Clearly, this story cannot be true for surely Allah, the Merciful, the Compassionate to humankind, would not provide detailed revelation and then omit an important practice such as the *adhan*.

Nonetheless, there exists another explanation, which is accepted by Shia scholars:[119]

> Gabriel came to the Prophet while the Prophet was resting on Ali. Gabriel read the *adhan* to them. To maintain this, the Prophet turned to Ali and said, "Did you hear the *adhan*?" Ali said, "Yes." The Prophet said, "Did you memorize it?" Ali said, "Yes." The Prophet said, "Then call Bilal; let us teach him the *adhan*." So they called Bilal and taught him the *adhan*.[120]

An important point to note is that because the instructions came from angel Gabriel, the *adhan* must be considered as being part of the revelation, and not a whimsical dream seen by one of the companions.

Prayer without *Taharah* (Ritual Purity)

Al-Bukhari narrates that one day a man came to Umar and said, "I am in a state of *janabah* (ritual impurity) and I cannot find water." Umar told him, "Do not pray." Ammar b. Yasir, who was sitting there retorted:

---

[119] *Wasail al-Shiah*, 4:612

[120] Prophet Muhammad said, "Ali, you can see all that I can see, and you can hear all that I can hear; except that you are not a prophet but a vicegerent and you are virtually on the path of virtue." *Nahjul Balaghah*, sermon 192

Do you not remember that you and I were in a battalion going to the battles, and both of us woke up and found ourselves in a state of ritual impurity, and we did not find water? So you did not pray, but I did the *tayammum* (ritual purification by means of dust) in the dust. We mentioned this to the Prophet, and the Prophet said that you should have put your hands in the dust and performed the *tayammum*.[121]

Primarily, the Qur'an prescribes the *tayammum* for situations when water cannot be found. (c. 4:43) Therefore, most of the Sunni schools of thought follow the Qur'an in this regard. Only the Hanafi school follows Umar's opinion and indicates that *tayammum* is permissible only while traveling or ill, but in all other cases, a person who cannot find water for *taharah* should not pray.

Tarawih Prayers

Al-Bukhari narrates from Abdullah b. Abd al-Qari:

I went with Umar b. al-Khattab during his period of caliphate one night in the Month of Ramadhan to the mosque. We saw the people praying scattered, not together. Umar said, "It is best if these people can pray together, and there is only one who leads the prayers." So he gathered them and appointed Ubay b. Ka'ab to lead the prayers. Another night, I went with Umar to the mosque and saw that the people were praying together, organized, and Umar said, "What an excellent innovation (*niam al-bidah hadhihi*)."[122]

Prayers for the Deceased

Although narrators like Ahmad b. al-Hanbal, al-Muslim, and al-Nisa'i all relate that the Prophet read prayers over the deceased with five *takbiraat*

---

[121] *Sunan al-Nisa'i*, 1:169; *Sunan Ibn Majah*, 1:188; Al-Bayhaqi, *Al-Sunan al-Kubaa*, 1:209; *Tafseer Ibn Katheer*, 4:505; Ibn Qudaamah, *Al-Mughni*, 1:234; Ibn Rushd, *Al-Bidayah wal-Nihayah*, 1:63

[122] *Sahih al-Bukaari*, 3:58; *Tarikh al-Madinah al-Munawarah*, 2:713; *Al-Riyadh al-Nadhirah*, 1:309; *Tarikh al-Yaqubi*, 2:114

(uttering "*Allahu akbar*");[123] however, Umar reduced the number of *takbiraat* in prayers over the deceased from five to four.[124]

Three Divorces in One Session

According to the Holy Qur'an (c. 2:229), a married couple may divorce each other three times before they are no longer allowed to remarry each other.[125] Thus, divorce must be declared and its rulings applied on three separate periods; the pronouncement of the three divorces cannot be declared in one declaration. The Holy Prophet explained:

> A man came to the Prophet and told him, "I divorced my wife." The Prophet asked, "How did you divorce her?" He said, "Three times in one session." The Prophet said, "That divorce is considered only one divorce. It cannot be considered three divorces, so you may take your wife back."[126]

However, historians say that divorce became more prevalent during the time of the second caliph; thus to make divorce easier, Umar allowed men to read all three pronouncements of divorce at one time.[127]

Other Actions performed by Umar

Umar also did following:

- Prevented the death announcement of the Prophet

- Objected to the Treaty of Hudaybiyyah

- Refused to join the dispatch of Usama as the Prophet commanded him to do so just before his death

---

[123] *Musnad Ahmad b. Hanbal*, 4:370; *Sahih al-Muslim, Baab al-Salat ala al-Qabr; Kitab al-Janazah*

[124] Al-Suyuti, *Tarikh al-Khulafah*, p. 137

[125] Al-Jassas, *Ahkam al-Qur'an*, 1:378

[126] *Sirat b. Ishaq*, 2:191

[127] *Sahih al-Muslim*, Chapter of *Talaq al-Thalath*, 1:575; *Musnad Ahmad b. Hanbal*, 1:314; Al-Bayhaqi, 7:336

- Prevented the Prophet from narrating his will

- He was the first person to give allegiance to Abu Bakr at Saqifah

- Offered two options to Ali and Fatima al-Zahra - pay allegiance to Abu Bakr or face the consequences

- Appointed Mu'awiyah as governor of Syria

- Appointed Abu Huraira as governor of Bahrain and then accused him of theft and lying about the statements of the Prophet

- Allocated different salaries to different groups of people, introducing discrimination into the financial system

- Permitted wiping over one's socks in *wudhu* instead of removing them and performing it on the bare feet;

- Prevented people from mourning over the dead[128]

- Forced people who had taken the names of prophets (as their first names) to change their names[129]

- Required all men to offer the same amount of *mahr* (marriage gift) to all women

Uthman b. al-Affan

According to Muslim historians, the third caliph Uthman b. al-Affan was assassinated because of his financial mismanagement and religious digression. The prominent historian Ibn Sa'd says that Uthman b. al-Affan governed for twelve years. For the first six years, he was very popular, but in the second six years, he brought his family members and clan to political power and flooded them with money, whereby he angered the people because those whom he appointed as administrators and governors over all the Islamic lands were corrupt.[130] Al-Tabari and

---

[128] *Umdat al-Qari*, 4:87; *Sahih al-Bukhari*, 2:102; *Sahih al-Muslim*, 2:238

[129] *Tabaqat b. Sa'd*, 5:51; *Umdat al-Qari*, 7:143

[130] Ibn Sa'd, *Al-Tabaqat al-Kubra*, 3:64

Ibn al-Atheer go further and agree that financial mismanagement was not the only reason why Uthman was killed; nonetheless, they say that they do not want to mention the other reasons because they do not want to stir the tension in the public.[131] Other sources are more vocal about what actually happened during that time.

Before assuming the caliphate, Uthman had agreed to follow the policies of his predecessors. However, after becoming the caliph, he reverted to the *jahiliyyah* practice of favoring his own relatives. Aware of Uthman's tendencies in that direction, Umar had previously warned him to refrain from nepotism because the people would reject it and the Quraysh would lose power,[132] however Uthman did not heed his advice.

Unlike Abu Bakr and Umar, Uthman filled the official positions with his own tribesmen, such as Abu Sufyan, Marwan b. al-Hakam, Mu'awiyah b. Abu Sufyan, al-Waleed b. Uqbah, Abdullah b. Abi Sarh, and Sa'ed b. al-Aas. In doing so, he angered many people, even those on the side of Quraysh, such as Lady Aishah.

Particularly upset were those who lost power due to Uthman's nepotism, such as Amr b. al-Aas, who lost Egypt; al-Mugheerah b. Shu'bah, who lost Kufa; and Abu Musa al-Ashari, who lost Basra. Adding insult to injury, Uthman then appointed incompetent and corrupt individuals from among the Bani Umayyah to fill those positions. As a result, some of those townships revolted and in Kufa for example, the people ousted Uthman's choice and reinstated Abu Musa al-Ashari.[133]

The administrative mismanagement began with al-Hakam b. al-Aas and his son Marwan. The Holy Prophet had exiled both of them from Madinah because they had been agitating the populace. During the caliphates of Abu Bakr and Umar, both leaders refused permission for them to return. However, when Uthman came to power, not only did he bring back al-Hakam b. al-Aas and Marwan, but he gave al-Hakam b. al-

---

[131] *Tarikh al-Tabari* 4:365; Ibn al-Atheer, *Al-Kamil fil-Tarikh*, 3:167

[132] Ibn al-Atheer, *Al-Kamil fil-Tarikh*, 3:67

[133] Ibn Sa'd, *al-Tabaqat*, 5:33

Aas 100,000 *dirhams*, and he gave his own daughter, Umme Aban in marriage to Marwan. As his son-in-law, Marwan became a close minister to Uthman and in turn, Uthman presented him with many gifts, such as allocating him all of the income of Africa. He even gave Marwan's brother Harith b. al-Hakam 300,000 *dirhams*.

Uthman favored his own relatives for government positions despite their incompetence, and in doing so, he alienated the rest of the Muslims, especially the Muhajireen and the Ansar. Rumor spread in the city of Kufa that Uthman wanted to honor his stepbrother at the expense of the ummah of Muhammad.[134]

In truth, Uthman replaced Sa'd b. Abi al-Waqqas, the well-liked governor of Kufa, with his step-brother al-Waleed b. Uqbah and thereby earned the wrath of the people, who asked whether it was just to replace Sa'd b. Abi al-Waqqas, whom they felt was moderate, kind, and forgiving with his own step-brother, who was in their words, "stupid, irreligious, and corrupt (*ahmaq, majin, wa fajir*)."[135]

He also allocated the entire income of Africa, from Tripoli to Tangiers, to another stepbrother, Ibn Abi Sarh and made him supreme governor of Egypt instead of governor of the countryside. In addition, he expanded the authority of Mu'awiyah b. Abu Sufyan, which had been limited to Damascus during the time of Umar, to include all of Shaam, which encompassed Syria, Jordan, Lebanon, Palestine, and other areas at that time. He treated others from the Bani Umayyah in a similar fashion.

These actions brought him into conflict with the people, not because they disliked the Bani Umayyah, but because those whom he appointed were dishonest and corrupt. However, when historians analyze the reasons behind Uthman's assassination, they say that it was not only because he departed from the egalitarian spirit of the Qur'an and allowed his clansmen to take from the people at a time of economic crisis and poverty, but that *bidah* (religious innovation) was a factor as well. Closer

---

[134] *Ansab al-Ashraf*, 5:32

[135] *Ansab al-Ashraf*, 5:30; Ibn Abil Hadid, *Sharh Nahjul-Balaghah*, 3:17

investigation of that period reveals that Uthman did in fact attempt to make changes to the religion.

Uthman's nepotism led to his assassination and the awaited succession of Ali b. Abi Talib to the caliphate. After Ali was murdered, power again shifted to the Quraysh group under the rule of Mu'awiyah b. Abu Sufyan. Learning from Uthman's errors, Mu'awiyah balanced political with tribal alliances and followed Umar's practice of appointing allies from outside his own tribe to official positions. Hence, Amr b. al-Aas, al-Mugheerah b. al-Shu'bah, Abu Huraira, al-Numan b. Basheer, and Abd al-Rahman b. Khalid all found places in the new caliphate under Mu'awiyah, and even Lady Aishah was pacified.

Al-Waleed b. Uqbah

One of the first examples of Uthman's mismanagement revolved around his stepbrother, al-Waleed b. Uqbah, whom Uthman made the governor of Kufa - much to the dismay of the people. Al-Waleed was habituated to drinking wine. One day when he was drunk, he came to the mosque to lead the prayers. After finishing two *rakats* (units of prayer), he turned to the people and asked, "Do you need more prayers?" One of the companions reproached him, "May the Lord never increase you in goodness, and neither the one who sent you as a governor over us (Uthman)," and then he threw a handful of pebbles in the face of al-Waleed. Others in the mosque followed suit, and al-Waleed drunkenly staggered back to the palace as the people stoned him.[136]

A group of Kufans went to Madinah to raise their grievances about al-Waleed b. Uqbah, but Uthman did not believe them and mocked them, so they went to the house of Lady Aishah. Aishah was furious at Uthman and told him, "You abandoned the tradition of the Prophet."[137] News of this incident spread and a crowd gathered in the Masjid of Madinah. Those who took Lady Aishah's side and those who took

---

[136] *Ansab al-Ashraf*, 5:32

[137] *Ansab al-Ashraf*, 5:34

Uthman's side fought and threw stones at each other. This day marked the first public fighting between Muslims in the city of Madinah since the death of the Prophet and this incident forced Uthman to replace his stepbrother with Sa'ed b. al-Aas as governor of Kufa in order to resolve the matter.

Known for his *fusuq* (impiety), Sa'ed b. al-Aas was no better than his predecessor and he treated Iraq as the personal property of the Quraysh, and in particular, the Bani Umayyah. One of those who opposed his governorship was Malik al-Ashtar al-Nakhai, but when he brought the issue up in public, more conflict ensued.[138] Others also objected to the practice of Sa'ed b. al-Aas that the public treasury (*bayt al-mal*) was wide open to the Bani Umayyah. Ali, Zubayr, Talha, Sa'd b. Abdullah, Abd al-Rahman b. Auf, and others came to Uthman to voice their objections to him, but Uthman rebuked them by saying, "This is my family and Allah has enjoined upon me to be kind to them."[139]

Uthman's Innovations

Third Call to Prayer (*Adhan*)

When the Messenger of Allah used to go to the mosque for the Friday prayers, the person in charge of giving the call to prayer would first call the *adhan* and then the *iqamah*, and this practice continued during the caliphates of Abu Bakr and Umar and for half of the caliphate of Uthman. However, in the seventh year of his caliphate, Uthman ordered that a third call to prayer be given. This shocked the Muslims[140] because they considered the addition of a third *adhan* to be a *bidah* (religious innovation).[141]

---

[138] *Ansab al-Ashraf*, 5:40; *Tarikh al-Tabari*, 4:322; *Kamil fil-Tarikh*, 3:137

[139] Al-Baladri, *Ansab al-Ashraf*, 5:25; Ibn Abil Hadid, *Sharh Nahjul-Balaghah*, 3:35

[140] *Ansab al-Ashraf*, 5:39; *al-Muntazam*, 5:7

[141] Ibn Abi Shaybah, *al-Musanaf*, 2:48; Al-Zuhai; and others

Al-Yaqubi comments in his history that Uthman had the audacity to climb the pulpit of the Prophet and sit in the same place that the Prophet used to sit in, even though Abu Bakr and Umar respected it by never sitting on the pulpit of the Prophet.[142]

Complete Prayers in Mina

During the Hajj (the Pilgrimage), the prayers in Mina used to be performed in the shortened version (*qasr*) by a person who was traveling. However, one year, Uthman recited the prayers in their full form rather than in their shortened form. Many of the companions protested and one of them, Abd al-Rahman b. Auf came to Uthman and asked, "Didn't you pray with the Prophet in this spot with two *rakats* (units of prayer)?" Uthman said he had. Abd al-Rahman b. Auf then asked, "Didn't you pray with Abu Bakr in this spot with two *rakats*?" Uthman said he had. Abd al-Rahman b. Auf further asked, "Didn't you pray with Umar in this spot with two *rakats*?" Uthman said that he had. Abd al-Rahman b. Auf continued, "Didn't you, yourself lead the prayers during your caliphate in this spot with two *rakats*?" Uthman said that he had. Abd al-Rahman then resorted to ask why Uthman had read the prayers with four *rakats* this time, to which Uthman replied, "I have married a woman from Mecca, and the people of Yemen came to me and said, Uthman is a resident of Mecca, but he still prays *qasr* even though he should pray the complete prayers; because of this, I wanted to do four *rakats*." Abd al-Rahman b. Auf then pointed out to him that the Holy Prophet himself was a resident of Mecca and he still led the prayers with two *rakats*, and that Uthman should follow the tradition of the Prophet. Uthman replied, "This is the opinion that I have followed."[143]

In another case, when Uthman was in Mina, he became ill and asked Ali b. Abi Talib to lead the prayers. Ali replied, "If you like, I will lead the prayers, but I will pray exactly the way that Prophet Muhammad did

---

[142] Al-Yaqubi, 2:162

[143] *Tarikh al-Tabari* 4:268; *Ansab al-Ashraf*, 5:39

(the shortened prayers)." Uthman objected and told him that he had to pray with four *rakats*, and the matter was left at that.

Khutbah before the Eid Prayer

Throughout the time of the Prophet and the caliphates of Abu Bakr and Umar, as well as today, the *khutbah* (sermon) on the day of Eid is said after the Eid Prayer. However, Uthman noticed that people tended to miss the prayers, so he developed the habit of giving the sermon first, and then after that leading the prayer.[144]

Land of Fadak and Marwan b. al-Hakam

Aside from encouraging Marwan b. al-Hakam to return from exile and making him his son-in-law, Uthman also granted him the land of Fadak.

Originally, the Prophet gave Fadak to his daughter Fatima al-Zahra because when the *ayah* of the Qur'an was revealed, "And give to your kin their right," (c. 17:26) the Angel Gabriel told the Prophet that he had to give Fadak to Fatima. However when Abu Bakr assumed the caliphate, he held that it was *fay* (income for all of the Muslim community), so he took Fadak away from her and made it a public endowment, while the Ahlul Bayt maintained that it was a private gift. Irrespective of which viewpoint one takes, Uthman still had no right to grant the land to a specific individual, since neither public endowments, nor private property of someone else can be given to a private party.

In addition to Fadak, as mentioned earlier, Uthman also gave Marwan all of the income from Africa. Such treatment raised discontent among the Muslims of Madinah because Marwan was not an admired or moral figure.

Reactions of Some Prominent Companions

On the account of Uthman's actions, many Muslims were not happy with him. The negative reaction of prominent Muslims is well

---

[144] Ibn Hajar, *Fath al-Bari*, 2:261

documented, and a careful review of this, may perhaps give some insight as to why Uthman was eventually assassinated.

Talha b. Abdullah said to Uthman, "You brought new innovations into the religion that people were unaware of before and did not know about in religion."[145]

Al-Zubayr b. al-Awam one day said about Uthman, "Kill him, he has changed your religion." The people reminded him that his own son stood at the door of Uthman and protected him. Al-Zubayr replied, "I would not dislike that Uthman be killed even if they start by killing my son."[146]

Abdullah b. Masud used to say about Uthman, "The best of truth is the Book of Allah, and the best guidance is the guidance of Muhammad, and the most evil things are the ones which have been innovated, and every new thing that has been brought up is *bidah*, and every *bidah* is deviation, and every deviant is in the Fire."[147]

Amaar b. Yasir, at the Battle of Siffeen, said that when the people were asked why they killed Uthman, they answered, "We killed him because of his *ihdath* (new innovations)."[148]

Sa'd b. Abi al-Waqqas was asked about the motivations behind Uthman's assassination and he said, "He changed - and he has been changed. He did good things and he did bad things. If we do good, then we have done good, and if we do bad then we ask forgiveness from Allah."[149]

Malik al-Ashtar describes Uthman in his letter to him as "the one who throws the injunctions of the Qur'an behind his back (*al-nabidh li*

---

[145] *Ansab al-Ashraf*, 5:29

[146] *Sharh Nahjul-Balaghah*, 9:36

[147] *Hayliyat al-Awliya, Sharh Nahjul-Balaghah*, 1:38; 3:42; *Ansab al-Ashraf*, 5:36

[148] *Kitab Siffeen*, 3:19

[149] *Al-Imamah wal-Siyasah*, 1:48

hukm al-Qur'an)," and "the one who has turned away from the tradition of the Prophet (*al-haid an sunnat al-Nabi*)."[150]

Lady Aishah, the wife of the Prophet said to Uthman, "How quickly you have deserted the tradition of your Prophet. His hair and his sandals have not yet decomposed" [the *sunnah* fell apart quicker than the remnants of the Holy Prophet]. She also said to him, "You have abandoned the tradition (*sunnah*) of the Messenger of Allah."[151]

Muhammad b. Abu Bakr, the son of the first caliph Abu Bakr, said to Uthman, "What religion do you follow?" Uthman replied, "I follow the religion of Islam," after which Muhammad told him, "You have changed the injunctions of the Book of Allah," and left angrily.[152]

Abu Dharr al-Ghifari, a close companion of the Prophet, said to Uthman, "By God, I have seen affairs and events that I cannot even recognize" [that they are neither in the Book of Allah, nor in the traditions of the Prophet]. He also said, "I can see truth which has been extinguished and falsehood (*batil*) which is being resurrected and an honest person whom people are doing wrong to and are saying that he is a liar."[153]

Such comments indicate that many prominent companions were displeased with Uthman's policies and his implementation of the Qur'an and the *sunnah*. The accusations they levied upon him, *bidah* and *ihdath* - both meaning innovation - are very serious in Islam. After he was killed, his body was left for three days - unwashed and unburied.[154] Finally, Marwan b. al-Hakam and three of his disciples recited the funeral prayers over him, but the people of Madinah, who had refused to participate in the funeral prayer stoned them. They did not allow his body to be buried in the same cemetery (as the Muslims), thus he was

---

[150] *Al-Futuh*, 1:40; *Ansab al-Ashraf*, 5:46

[151] *Ansab al-Ashraf*, 5:48; *Al-Futuh*, 1:64; *Sharh Nahjul-Balaghah*, 3:49

[152] *Al-Tabaqat*, 3:73; *Al-Bidayah wal-Nihayah*, 7:193; *Al-Kamil*, 3:178; *Al-Imamah wal-Siyasah*, 1:44

[153] *Ansab al-Ashraf*, 5:53; *Sharh Nahjul-Balaghah*, 3:55

[154] *Ansab al-Ashraf*, 5:83; *al-Muntazam*, 5:58

buried outside the boundaries of the al-Baqi cemetery. Later on, when Mu'awiyah b. Abu Sufyan took power, he extended al-Baqi to include the grave of Uthman.

An Analysis of Uthman's Motivations

For the first six years of his caliphate, Uthman followed the precedents of the first two caliphs. At some point however, he realized that the people did not view him as his own entity; but rather as a follower of the *Shaykhayn* (Abu Bakr and Umar b. al-Khattab) and he felt that he was not receiving the respect that his position entitled him to.

The people had permitted Umar b. al-Khattab to alter the religion based on circumstances, such as when Umar expanded the grounds of Masjid al-Haram (the Ka'abah), or increased the government subsidies (*aba*). However, they did not give Uthman the same level of tolerance and flexibility, even though Uthman, like Umar, was tied by blood to the Holy Prophet.

Even when he tried to expand the sacred mosque (in Madinah) as Umar had done, the people said, "He expands the mosque of the Prophet, but he changes his tradition." According to al-Tabari, when Uthman demolished the homes around the sacred mosque for its expansion, he attempted to compensate their owners, but they refused to accept the money. Uthman said to them, "Do you know what made you strong in front of me and made you accuse me? It was my forbearance. Umar did exactly the same thing to you, but you did not protest."[155]

He said to others, "You accuse me of things that happened during the time of Umar b. al-Khattab, but you did not accuse him. You agreed with him, and he forced you to follow him and his tradition; whereas I gave you freedom and freedom of expression, and I barred my hands and my tongue from you, and that is what gave you the courage to attack me."[156]

---

[155] *Tarikh al-Tabari*, 4:251

[156] *Tarikh al-Tabari*, 4:339

Overall, Uthman lacked the strength to resist the desire for fame and recognition and new ideas in his name.

Chapter 10
The Ummah Fractures

﴿فَتَقَطَّعُوا أَمْرَهُم بَيْنَهُمْ زُبُرًا كُلُّ حِزْبٍ بِمَا لَدَيْهِمْ فَرِحُونَ﴾

But people have cut off their affair (of unity), between them into sects: each party rejoices in that which is with itself.

Holy Qur'an, 23:53

The tumult of the Quraysh group could not leave the Muslim ummah unscathed. Although the popular viewpoint today is that Islam has maintained two sects—Sunni and Shia, but the fact of the matter is that virtually hundreds of Muslim religious sects came and went in the past.

Nonetheless, the fracture, which has grown into the two main paths (Sunni and Shia) cannot be neglected. Many bystanders view the Shia aspect of Islam as a deviation from the norm and a split from the "original Islam" because the Shia are a minority. However, the Shia maintain that their path is actually the original and unaltered version of Islam as taught by the Prophet, and verified and secured by his family (Ahlul Bayt).

When did Shiaism Come About?

Historians vary as to when the term "Shia" came into being. Some Sunni sources say that "Shia Islam" emerged at the time of the death of the Prophet, while others say that it took form afterwards. Some Sunni historians also differ as to the influence of Shia Islam, with some citing a fringe band following a legendary figure named Abdullah b. Saba. However, the Shia say otherwise and affirm that the concept of "Shia" was entitled as the "Shia of Ali" by the Prophet during his lifetime, and that it was a real force in Islamic history that took form and was shaped by the Qur'an and the *sunnah*.

Interpreters of the Qur'an assert that when the following verse was revealed to the Prophet, "Verily, those who believe and do good deeds: they are the best of creation," the Prophet then turned and pointed to Ali and said, "This man and his Shia (followers) are the best of creation."[1]

As the Muslim community expanded, the Prophet continued to refer to some of the Muslims as the "Shia of Ali." Al-Suyuti, a Sunni scholar narrates on the authority of Jabir b. Abdullah al-Ansari:

> We were sitting with the Prophet when Ali came. The Prophet said, "By the One who has my soul in His hands, verily this man (he pointed to Ali) and his friends (*shia*) will be the successful ones on the Day of Judgment."[2 & 3]

This hadith is related in several similar versions in the books of hadith compiled by Sunni scholars. In addition, some Sunni scholars have recorded that during the time of the Prophet, some of the companions were distinguished from others as being the "Shia of Ali." They included Abu Dharr al-Ghifari, Ammar b. Yasir, al-Miqdaad b. al-Aswad, and Salman al-Farsi. Therefore, saying that the term Shia emerged after the death of the Prophet is incorrect, since the first person to introduce the concept of "Shia" was the Prophet himself during his own lifetime.

One of the key differences between the Shia and non-Shia interpretations of Islam is the right to succession after the death of the Prophet, thus the misconception that Shiaism emerged after the death of

---

[1] *Holy Qur'an*, 98:7

[2] Al-Suyuti, *Al-Durr al-Manthur*, 6:376

[3] *Inna hadha wa shiatuhu la-hum al-faizun yawm al-qiyamah.*

the Prophet is understandable. Early Sunni historians, such as Ibn Khaldun and al-Yaqubi, as well as contemporary academics, such as Egyptian scholars Dr. Hasan Ibrahim and Dr. Ahmad Amin, have expressed the following viewpoints on the successorship of the Prophet. Ibn Khaldun and al-Yaqubi contend that the Shia began as a group of companions who were the friends of Ali b. Abi Talib, and hence supported the claim that the chosen family members of the Prophet, known as Ahlul Bayt have the right of leadership.[4] Al-Yaqubi also specifies a group of companions who refused to pay allegiance to Abu Bakr as being: Salman al-Farsi, Abu Dharr al-Ghifari, al-Miqdaad b. al-Aswad, and al-Abbas b. Abdul Muttalib.[5] Dr. Hasan Ibrahim[6] and Dr. Ahmad Amin[7] focus on the same concept, with Dr. Amin contending that Ali was seen as having the right to leadership on account of his nearness to the Prophet and his own personal merits.

However, Dr. Amin then advances the idea that although Shiaism began with the straightforward disagreement of the first three appointed caliphs, elements from Judaism, Christianity, and the Magians (the religion of the ancient Persians) caused it to deviate. He argues that since the Persians were forced to convert, they left the biggest footprints of their heritage on Shia Islam. However, this argument is not warranted.

To begin with, the majority of the new converts including the Persians followed the Sunni interpretation of Islam. Another important point is that it was not until the fifteenth century AD that Persia became a Shia nation. It is known that all of the Twelve Imams of the Shia are full-blooded Arabs from Quraysh (as the hadith from the Prophet said they would be), and the Shia, like the rest of the Muslims, are a mixture of Arab and non-Arab people. Muslims who come from non-Arab cultures enrich Islam as a whole in their own unique ways; thus, that

---

[4] *Tarikh Ibn Khaldun,* 3:364

[5] *Tarikh al-Yaqubi,* 2:104

[6] Dr. Hasan Ibrahim, *Tarikh al-Islam,* 1:371

[7] Dr. Ahmad Amin, *Fajr al-Islam,* 266

influence is not limited to Shiaism, and many of the great scholars and narrators of the Sunni tradition, such as al-Bukhari come from non-Arab countries. Hence, the argument that Shiaism developed because of the influence of non-Islamic ideas, is in essence nothing more than a faulty attempt to marginalize the role of Shiaism in the Islamic history.

Some Sunni sources speculate Shia Islam emerged in the time between the death of the Prophet and the martyrdom of Imam Husayn in Karbala. Sunni historian Ibn Hazm suggested that Shiaism could have come about during the time of Uthman, while another Sunni historian, al-Nawbakhti and others say that Shiaism took form during the caliphate of Ali b. Abi Talib, specifically during the Battle of the Camel in Basra.[8] Still, a few others maintain that while the spiritual side of Shiaism developed after the death of the Prophet, the political dimension of Shiaism was born after the martyrdom of Imam Husayn.

In contrast, the majority of the Shia scholars hold that Shiaism first appeared in Mecca during the early stage of the prophethood of the last Messenger when Allah revealed the verse, "And warn your relatives of nearest kin."[9] After this verse was revealed, the Holy Prophet invited forty members of his tribe (Bani Hashim) for a meal with him in the house of his uncle Abu Talib and then he informed them about his prophethood and asked who would support him. None responded except for Ali b. Abi Talib. The Holy Prophet repeated the question three times, but still none responded except Ali. At that time, the Holy Prophet put his hand on the shoulder of Ali and declared, "This is my brother, my legatee, and my successor (*khalifah*) over you, so listen to him and obey him." The invited relatives laughed and teased the father of Ali because the Prophet had ordered him to obey his son.[10] Therefore,

---

[8] *Firaq al-Shiah*, p.16; Ibn al-Nadeem, *Al-Fihrist*, p.175

[9] *Holy Qur'an*, 26:214

[10] *Ihqaq al-Haqq*, 4:62; *Tarikh al-Tabari*, 2:117; *Musnad Ahmad b. Hanbal*, 1:159; *Tarikh Abul Fida*, 1:116; *Nadhm Durar al-Simtayn*, p.82; *Kifayat al-Talib*, p.205; *Tarikh Madinat Dimishq*, 1:87, hadith 139 & 143; Al-Hasakani, *Shawahid al-Tanzil*, 1:420; Muhammad b. Jarir al-Tabari, *Jami al-Bayan*, 19:131; Jalal al-Din al-Suyuti, *Al-Durr al-Manthur*, 5:97; *Tafseer b. Kathir*, 3:350;

according to the Shia, all Muslims were ordered to follow Ali b. Abi Talib after the Holy Prophet; therefore, the subtle divide between those who did so willingly, and those who did not, marked the first definition of Shia.

Why the Focus on Ahlul Bayt?

Qur'anic Verse on those who Possess Knowledge

Many Muslims often cite the Qur'anic verse - repeated twice - that instructs, "Ask those who possess knowledge if you do not know."[11] Since both Sunni and Shia commentators explain that "those who possess knowledge" refers to the Prophet, Ali, Fatima, Hasan, and Husayn,[12] hence the Shia stance has always maintained that all religious questions and interpretations of the Qur'an must be referred to them.

The Verse of Purity (*Ayat al-Tatheerah*)

"Allah only wishes to remove all uncleanliness away from you, Ahlul Bayt, and to purify you completely." (c. 33:33) In his *tafseer* (exegesis), the reputable Sunni, al-Fakhr al-Razi uses this *ayah* (verse) to prove that those five individuals (the Prophet, Ali, Fatima, Hasan, and Husayn) have been purified and immune from any form of sin, both major and minor.

This *ayah* (c. 33:33) descended in the house of Umme Salamah, one of the wives of the Prophet, which later was referred to as the "Event of the Cloak (*Hadith al-Kisa*)." When the *ayah* was revealed, the Prophet, Ali b.

Al-Baghdadi, *Tafseer al-Khazin*, 3:371; Al-Alusi al-Baghdadi, *Ruh al-Maani*, 19:122; Al-Tantawi, *Tafseer al-Jawahir*, 13:103; Al-Hakim al-Naysaburi, *Al-Mustadrak ala al-Sahihayn*, 3:135. Other historical sources, such as *Sirat al-Halabi*, say that the Holy Prophet added, "And he will be my minister (*wazir*) and inheritor (*warith*)."

[11] *Holy Qur'an*, 16:43 & 21:7

[12] *Tafseer al-Tabari*, 14:109; Al-Alusi, *Tafseer Ruh al-Maani*, 14:134; *Tafseer al-Qurtubi*, 11:272; *Tafseer Ibn al-Katheer*, 2:570; Al-Hakim, *Tafseer Shawahid al-Tanzel*, 1:334; *Tafseer al-Thalabi*

Abi Talib, Fatima, Hasan, and Husayn were gathered beneath a cloak, and the Angel Gabriel directed and included this *ayah* to all of them. Umme Salamah was present and asked the Prophet whether she could join them too, but he softly refused her saying, "*Anti ala khayr* (You are from the people of good)." Therefore, the wives of the Prophet were not included as part of the "Ahlul Bayt" in this *ayah*, as some assume. To prove further, another wife of the Prophet, Lady Aishah narrated herself that the only people concerned in this verse were Prophet Muhammad, Ali, Fatima, Hasan, and Husayn.

Although, the beginning verses of 33:33 (*ayah*) address the wives of the Prophet, the ending verses (*ayah*) clearly do not, since they refer to "Ahlul Bayt" in the mixed (masculine and feminine) gender, rather than in the strict feminine gender, which is used when referring exclusively to the wives of the Prophet (as it was in the beginning). Since the Qur'an is written in Arabic, the language is extraordinarily rich in its linguistic composition and it uses the precise words, structure, and style to express itself clearly.

﴿وَقَرْنَ فِي بُيُوتِكُنَّ وَلَا تَبَرَّجْنَ تَبَرُّجَ الْجَاهِلِيَّةِ الْأُولَى وَأَقِمْنَ الصَّلَاةَ وَآتِينَ الزَّكَاةَ وَأَطِعْنَ اللَّهَ وَرَسُولَهُ إِنَّمَا يُرِيدُ اللَّهُ لِيُذْهِبَ عَنكُمُ الرِّجْسَ أَهْلَ الْبَيْتِ وَيُطَهِّرَكُمْ تَطْهِيرًا﴾

And stay quietly in your houses, and make not a dazzling display, like that of the former times of Ignorance; and establish regular prayer, and give regular charity; and obey Allah and His Messenger [*in Arabic this portion is written in the strictly feminine form*]. And Allah only wishes to remove all abomination from you, O members of the Family, and to make you pure and immaculate [*this portion is written in the masculine form, implying its direction to a mixed gender*].[13]

Nonetheless, some still argue that "Ahlul Bayt" also included others; but, according to Shia scholars (who are unanimous on this issue) and at least twenty-four prominent Sunni historical references state that this *ayah* refers exclusively to Prophet Muhammad, Ali, Fatima, Hasan, and Husayn. The Sunni historians include:

1. *Sahih al-Muslim*, Fadhail Ahlul Bayt 2:368

2. *Al-Khasais* of al-Imam al-Nisa'i, 49

3. *Sahih al-Tirmidhi*, 5:30

4. *Musnad Ahmad b. al-Hanbal*, 1:330

5. *Al-Sawaiq al-Muhraqah*, Ibn Hajar al-Asqalani, 85

6. *Al-Estiaab*, Ibn Abd al-Birr, 3:37

7. *Tafseer al-Qurtubi*, 14:182

8. *Ahkam al-Qur'an*, Ibn Arabi, 2:166

9. *Mustadrak al-Hakim*, 3:123

10. *Asbaab al-Nuzul al-Wahidi*, 203

11. *Muntakhib Kanz al-Umal*, 5:96

12. *Al-Bukhari, Al-Tarikh al-Kabeer*, 1:69

13. *Tafseer al-Fakh al-Razi*, 2:700

14. *Al-Seerah al-Halabiyah*, 3:212

15. *Usd al-Ghabah*, Ibn al-Atheer, 2:12

16. *Tafseer al-Tabari*, 22:6

17. *Tarikh Ibn Asakir*, 1:185

---

[13] *Holy Qur'an*, 33:33

18. *Tafseer al-Kashshaf*, al-Zamakhshari, 1:193

19. *Manaqib al-Khawarizmi*, 23

20. *Al-Seerah al-Dahlaniyyah*, 3:329

21. *Tafseer b. Katheer*, 3:483

22. *Al-Aqd al-Fareed*, Ibn Abd Rabah, 4:311

23. *Masabih al-Sunnah*, al-Baghawi, 2:278

24. *Al-Durr al-Manthur*, al-Suyuti, 5:198

The Verse of Malediction (*Ayat al-Mubahilah*)

The verse known as the *"Mubahilah"* (malediction) proposes, "Say (O Prophet) come, let us summon our sons and your sons and our women and your women, and ourselves and yourselves, and then let us invoke the curse of God upon the liars." (c. 3:61) The revelation is directed towards the Christians of Najran who disputed the claim of the Holy Prophet's prophethood and the nature of Jesus (whether he was divine or a prophet).

After the revelation of this verse, a meeting was arranged between the Muslims and the Christians under the conditions of the *ayah* in which both sides would solemnly swear to invoke the curse of Allah upon the side that was wrong.

The Christians brought along their hierarchy of priests to the malediction, however when they arrived, they found that the Prophet had brought only himself, his son-in-law and cousin, Ali; his daughter, Fatima; and his two grandsons, Hasan and Husayn. No one else, not even his wives were present even though the *ayah* had said "our women and your women."

Although confident of his prophethood, the Prophet took with him the dearest of all people to him - his family - because he wanted the Christians to witness the seriousness of the malediction by which he was even ready to put his own family at risk when it came to defending Islam and his message. Seeing that the Prophet was willing to endanger those closest to him and put them face to face with the wrath of God, the Christians became fearful. The leader of the Christians, Zamakhshari, said, "O Christians! I am beholding such faces that if God wishes, for their sake, He would move mountains for them. Do not accept their challenge for malediction, for if you do, you will all perish and no Christian will remain on the face of the earth until the Day of Resurrection."[14]

The mutual malediction was aborted and the Christians retreated to Najran, but later returned to embrace Islam.

Status of the Ahlul Bayt

The author of *Sahih al-Bukhari* narrates that a group of Muslims came to the Prophet and asked him, "O Messenger of Allah, Allah has ordered us to send our prayers upon you, so how should we send our prayers upon you?" (Referring to the verse 33:56 in the Holy Qur'an where Allah says, "Indeed Allah and His angels bless the Prophet; O you who have faith! Invoke blessings on him and invoke Peace upon him in a worthy manner." The Prophet replied, "Say, 'O Allah, bless Muhammad and the family of Muhammad, just as you blessed Ibrahim and the family of Ibrahim, and grant favor to Muhammad and the family of Muhammad, just as you granted favor to Ibrahim and the family of Ibrahim; truly, You the most Praiseworthy and Noble One in the worlds.'"[15]

Sanctity of the Ahlul Bayt

In the battlefield of the Battle of Uhud, on the day when the Messenger of Allah was hit on his forehead and was injured, he raised his head in supplication and said, "The wrath of Allah increased upon the Jews when they attributed Uzayr to Him and said that Uzayr was the son of

---

[14] *Tafseer al-Kashshaf*

[15] *Allahumma salli ala Muhammadin wa aale Muhammad kama sallayta ala Ibrahim wa aale Ibrahim, wa barik ala Muhammadin wa aale Muhammad kama barakta ala Ibrahim wa aale Ibrahim fil-aalameena innaka hamidun majeed.*

Allah; and His wrath increased upon the Christians when they attributed divinity to Jesus and said that the Messiah was the son of God; and His wrath increased upon those people who made my blood flow and those who annoy my family members."[16]

Ahlul Bayt - According to the Prophet

The Messenger of Allah said, "The parable of my household among you is the parable of the ark of Nuh (Noah); whoever embarked upon that ship was saved, and whoever did not was drowned (*Mathalu ahl al bayti fikum ka-mathali safeenati Nuh*)."[17]

The Messenger of Allah said, "We are members of a family that no one can ever be compared to (*Nahnu ahl baytin laa yuqassu binaa ahad*)."[18]

Rafidah (The Rejecters)

In recent years, the term *rafidah* (rejecters) has been increasingly used to refer to the Shia on account of their refusal to recognize the first three caliphs as legitimate. This term "*rafidah*" dates back to the Umayyah time and was used as a derogatory term to insult the Shia.[19]

Imam al-Shafi'i composed a famous line of poetry regarding this subject in which he said, "If *rafidah* be the love of the family of Muhammad, then let the *jinn* (spirits) and mankind bear witness that I am a *rafidah*."[20]

---

[16] Al-Muttaqi al-Hindi, *Kanz al-Umal*, 10:435, hadith 30050

[17] *Kanz al-Umal* 6:216; *Mustadrak al-Sahihayn*, 2:343; Al-Tabarani, *Al-Mujam al-Kabeer*, 12:27; Ibn Hajar, *Al-Sawaiq al-Muhriqah*, 1:86

[18] *Kunuz al-Haqaiq*, 153; *Al-Riyadh al-Nadhirah*, 2:208

[19] Al-Zubaydi, *Taj al-Arus*, 5:35; Al-Jawhari, 3:1078

[20] *In kana rafdhan hubbu aale Muhammadin. Fal yashhad al-thaqalan anni rafidahi.*

How "Shia Islam" Originated

"Shia Islam" originated based on love for the family of the Prophet, not the hatred of some around him. Although some Shia individuals may have said some unbecoming remarks about the first two caliphs, their comments cannot be taken to represent the views of all Shia. In fact, Ali b. Abi Talib forbade his followers from verbally abusing those who fought him[21] and this principle is in line with the Book of Allah which commands, "Abuse yet not those whom they invoke besides God, lest they abuse God in transgression without knowledge; thus have We made fair-seeming to every people their deeds."[22]

Nonetheless, despite the exhortations of the Ahlul Bayt, defamation and prosecution against the Shia occurred by those who opposed them. Perhaps it was a natural reaction to the conditions set by the Umayyah rule. For instance, Mu'awiyah b. Abu Sufyan bribed and forced all the leaders of the Friday Prayer (*Salat al-Jumah*) to curse Imam Ali, Hasan, Husayn, and Fatima al-Zahra - for over forty years. However, when Umar b. Abd al-Aziz came to power, he attempted to stop this practice, but it had become so firmly entrenched that his efforts were futile.

Moreover, asides from having to endure the continuous unjust slandering of the closest family members of the Prophet who are revered by Shia and non-Shia Muslims alike, the followers of Ahlul Bayt were severely tortured during the Umayyah and Abbasid time for their loyalty.

Abdullah b. Saba: Myth or Reality?

Over the centuries, a preposterous idea developed that the Shia doctrine originated from a Jewish man who hated Islam and infiltrated the Muslims to destroy them. His name is said to have been Abdullah b. Saba. However, some contemporary Sunni scholars, Shia scholars, Western authors, and a logical study of the background of this invented figure all concur that Abdullah b. Saba never even existed.

---

[21] *Nahjul Balaghah*

[22] *Holy Qur'an*, 6:108

None of the important primary Sunni sources such as al-Baladri and Ibn Sa'd even mention Ibn Saba; only al-Tabari mentions him, but the accounts of Ibn Saba are given on the authority of two extremely unreliable men: Sayf b. Umar al-Tamimi and al-Sari b. Yahya. Sunni narrators, such as Ibn Hayyan, Ibn Uday, and Ibn Muin all confer that Sayf b. Umar al-Tamimi forged or mistook hadith. Similarly, in the following books: *al-Tahdheeb, Mizan al-Itidal,* and *Tadhkirat al-Mawdhuat* they mention two men referred to as al-Sari (al-Sari b. Ismail al-Hamdani al-Kufi and al-Sari b. Asim al-Hamdani) who lived during the time of al-Tabari (who is most likely the al-Sari mentioned earlier by al-Tabari), who were renowned for fabricating hadiths.[23]

However, a different al-Sari, whose hadiths were reliable lived much before them - he died in 167 AH, therefore al-Tabari, who was born in 224 AH could never have met him. Since all of the subsequent sources that discuss Ibn Saba refer back to the history of al-Tabari and the information given by al-Tabari was at best questionable, hence more than likely, the existence of Ibn Saba was concocted by the two dishonest men (Sayf b. Umar al-Tamimi and al-Sari b. Yahya).[24]

Nonetheless, whether true or fictional, the information that al-Tabari provides regarding Ibn Saba is worth examining.

According to al-Tabari, Ibn Saba was a Jewish man who came from Sana in Yemen. His mother's name was Sawda, and he is said to have become a Muslim during the caliphate of Uthman. He traveled throughout the Muslim countries from Hijaz, Basra, Shaam, and Egypt, all the while propagating the notion that just like Prophet Isa will have a second coming, so too will Prophet Muhammad, citing c. 28:85 as a roundabout sort of evidence, "Indeed He who has revealed to you the Qur'an will surely restore you to the place of return. Say, 'My Lord knows best him who brings guidance and him who is in manifest error.'"

---

[23] *Lisan al-Mizan,* 3:12; *al-Ghadir,* 8:143

[24] *Al-Ghadir,* 9:218

However, some modern historians, such as Muhammad Fareed Wajdi in his encyclopedia *Dairat al-Marif*, not only added more fiction to al-Tabari's accounts, but also told a slightly different version. Wajdi maintained that Ibn Saba was a close follower of Imam Ali and admired him so much that he attributed divinity to him. According to this fable, when Imam Ali heard Ibn Saba's claim he wanted to take his life, but at the advice of Abdullah b. Abbas he sent Ibn Saba to al-Madain instead. This reaction is incidentally in complete disagreement with what is known about the behavioral pattern of Imam Ali, who is recorded to have spared an enemy out of fear that he might be killing him out of anger rather than out of justice.

Al-Wajdi continues that while in al-Madain, Ibn Saba is said to have spread the first notion that Ali was a prophet and later that he was a deity.[25] Other contemporary authors, such as Ahmad Atayllah, declare that Ibn Saba wanted to weaken and destroy the caliphate of Uthman, thus he intentionally mixed some Jewish ideas with Islam to form the doctrines about the return of the Prophet (*raja*) and the knowledge of Imam Ali about the unseen (*ilm al-ghayb*, which by definition is that which is known by no one).[26]

By attributing these ideas to Ibn Saba, real or imaginary, these authors not only succeeded in discrediting the Shia and presenting the Shia ideology as nothing more than imported teachings from another religion (instead of a legitimate and integral part of the history of Islam), but they also shifted the blame for the assassination of Uthman to some unorthodox sectarian incident, rather than on the administrative policies of Uthman, which bred so much resentment that he was killed - not by followers of "Ibn Saba," but by the companions of the Prophet.

The idea that someone with Ibn Saba's heretical mentality convinced the Muslims, many of whom were companions and who had seen the Prophet firsthand, is ludicrous. Even more unrealistic is the idea that

---

[25] Wajdi, Muhammad Fareed; *Dairat al-Marif al-Qarn al-Aishren*, 5:17

[26] Atayllah, Ahmad; *Al-Qamus al-Islami*, 3:222

someone so powerful who was able to bring down the third caliphate, could have existed unmentioned at such a heavily scrutinized time, even well after he had passed away.

It is also unconceivable to believe that Uthman, who severely punished some of the companions of the Prophet, such as Ammar b. Yasir and Ibn Masud, over issues unrelated to Islamic doctrine, would overlook such a person, since he could have been a potential threat to topple his power structure.

Furthermore, even the scant narratives regarding Ibn Saba conflict with one another because some people said that he appeared during the time of Uthman, while others said that he appeared during the lifetime of Imam Ali, and still others said that he came on the scene after the death of Ali. Even more, some said that he just revered Imam Ali, while others said that his main goal was to turn popular opinion against Uthman.

For these reasons, the Shia scholars, who have studied this subject in depth; as well as many orientalists, such as Bernard Lewis, Wellhausen, Friedlander, and others all agree that Ibn Saba was nothing but a legend fabricated by those who came later on in history.

The myth of Ibn Saba did not develop out of a vacuum. At the time when stories about him first spread, the status quo was threatened by the fact that the beliefs of Shia Islam, which are based firmly on the Qur'an, the *sunnah* of the Prophet, and the appointment of successors by the Prophet. Inventing Ibn Saba and attributing the ideas of Shia Islam to him in a much-skewed fashion made the Shia appear more as a fringe group rather than as part of the Islamic core. As the Egyptian scholar Taha Husayn says in his book *Al-Fitnah al-Kubra*, "The opponents of the Shia exaggerated the issue of Ibn Saba in order to defame Ali and his followers. Ibn Saba was an imaginary figure (*shakhsiyah wahmiyah*), and the only source that mentioned him was Sayf b. Umar, and he was a man well known to be a liar."[27]

---

[27] Taha Husayn, *Al-Fitnah al-Kubra*, the chapter on Ibn Saba.

More about Ibn Saba can be found in the book of Taha Husayn or in the thesis of Sayyid Murtadha al-Askari.[28]

Four Schools of Thought

Another misconception is that Islam, outside of the Shia school of thought, crystallized directly into four schools of thought, whereas in reality, the process was more complicated than this. However, through a combination of factors, not the least of which was government supported, these schools coalesced and took on separate identities during the time of the Abbasid Empire (75 AH - 1258).

Hanafi School (Al-Madhab al-Hanafi)

The Hanafi school, founded by Imam Abu Hanifah al-Nu'man b. Thabit (80 - 148 AH), was the first to acquire widespread popularity.

The first scholar to pay allegiance to this school of thought was Abul Abbas al-Saffah who was the leader of the revolution against the Umayyah dynasty and the founder of the Abbasid Empire. Other scholars and jurists (*fuqaha*) also joined him in the hope that a just government would rise and implement the *sunnah* of the Prophet and save the Muslim ummah from the tyranny of the Umayyah dynasty. However, Abu Hanifah soon realized that the Abbasid were not sincere in their call to establish the Islamic *sharia* (law) and Islamic government, and so he distanced himself from the government and refused to accept the formidable position of leadership in the judiciary system (*al-qada*) during the time of al-Mansur al-Abbasi.

Al-Mansur tried to bring Abu Hanifah to his side, but he refused and was then imprisoned, and according to some accounts even tortured. Some historians have also reported that the Abbasid eventually poisoned Abu Hanifah.

---

[28] His work on Abdullah b. Saba is available in English under the title of *Abdullah Ibn Saba and Other Myths* and has been printed in two volumes.

Nonetheless, the Abbasid government succeeded in attracting two of the most prominent students who had studied directly under Abu Hanifah: Abu Yusuf al-Qadi and Muhammad b. al-Hasan al-Shaybani. Abu Yusuf joined the Abbasid government during the reign of al-Mahdi al-Abbasi in the year 158 AH. He continued working for them during the rules of al-Hadi and al-Rashid and wrote several works on jurisprudence, one of the most noteworthy being *Kitab al-Kharaj*, which he wrote at the request of the caliph Harun al-Rashid.

He enjoyed an intimate relationship with the ruling powers, and through this, they supplemented the salary they paid him with gifts and lavish invitations, enabling him to lead an extravagant life for that time.

The other student, Muhammad b. al-Hasan al-Shaybani, assumed leadership of the judiciary system (*al-qada*) during the time of Harun al-Rashid. He wrote many thesis in jurisprudence (*fiqh*), including *Jami al-Sagheer*, which he narrated from Abu Yusuf al-Qadi, Abu Hanifah, and Jami al-Kabeer.[29]

Undoubtedly, the government played a central role in promoting the Hanafi school of thought because of Abu Yusuf al-Qadi and Muhammad b. al-Hasan al-Shaybani, and particularly since the position of judiciary leadership that the latter took, was central in promoting the jurisprudence (*fiqh*) of a particular school of thought. Regarding this issue, Ibn Hazm says:

> Two schools of thought were promoted and spread in the beginning of their emergence by leadership (*riyasah*) and the government (*sultanah*). The first was the Hanafi school of thought; since Abu Yusuf al-Qadi was declared the leader of the high court, he employed people only from his school of thought. The second school of thought that was supported by the government was the Maliki school of thought.[30]

---

[29] Al-Zarakli, *Al-Alam*, 6:80

[30] *Wafayat al-Ayan*, 6:144

Along the same line, al-Dahlawi says:

> Any school of thought whose leaders are famous and who assumed the
> positions of judiciary leadership (*qada*) and authority (*ifta* or the *fatwa*)
> will spread among the lands and expand day after day. Conversely, the
> people will not know any school of thought whose leaders did not
> assume the position of judiciary leadership and authority, and they will
> die out in the future.[31]

From this, it is clear that the expansion of a school of thought at that
time, hinged on the government. The government in turn, supported the
schools of thought because of their willingness to compromise Islamic
principles in favor of the government, and so a reciprocal relationship
developed between the government and the propagators of the schools
of thought who used the judiciary positions (the position of *qadi*) that
they were appointed to, to spread their ideologies to the masses.

Maliki School of Thought (*Al-Madhab al-Maliki*)

Once Al-Mansur al-Abbasi failed to sway Abu Hanifah to his side, he
turned his attention towards Imam Malik b. Anas (93 - 179 AH) and
proposed that the body of Islamic knowledge unify under one definitive
book and set of guidelines, rather than be split among several schools of
thought, as was the case at that time. He encouraged Imam Malik to
write *al-Muwatta* (the book that Imam Malik is well-known for). History
says:

> Al-Mansur spoke to al-Malik around 150 AH and encouraged him to
> write *Fiqh al-Muwatta*. He told him, "Put down this knowledge in
> writing, and try to avoid the eccentricity (*shawad*) of Ibn Abdullah al-
> Masud, the leniency (*rukhsah*) of Ibn Abbas, and the harshness (*shadaid*)
> of Ibn Umar. Be moderate in this *fiqh* and write whatever the majority
> of the *imams* and *sahabah* agree upon, and we promise you that we will

---

[31] Al-Dahlawi, *Hujjat Allah al-Balighah*, 1:151

bring all the people to follow your school of thought, and your *fiqh* and your knowledge, and we will spread and promote your book in the provinces and states, and we will ask the people not to oppose it, and they will not give judgments other than those in accordance with your books."[32]

Imam Malik spent approximately 11 years writing *al-Muwatta*, and his book eventually became the definitive legal text of the Abbasid state. The Abbasid rulers in turn, exhibited the utmost respect towards Imam Malik to the extent that Harun al-Rashid would stand whenever he saw Imam Malik, and then sit on the floor in front of him to listen to what he had to say. Through his open support of al-Mansur, Imam Malik alienated his teacher Rabiat al-Rai who refused to compromise his principles for the government and then parted company with Imam Malik.

Imam Malik continued to support the Abbasid government beyond the reign of al-Mansur into the time of al-Mahdi al-Abbasi. Just like al-Mansur, al-Mahdi al-Abbasi succeeded not in winning over the support of the Hanafi school of thought, but to entice two of Abu Hanifah's most famous students (as mentioned above).

At the same time, as they fostered the growth of the Maliki movement, the Abbasid also attempted to suppress the school of Ahlul Bayt. Not only were the ideas of Ahlul Bayt school threatening, but its leaders were also popular, such as Imam Ja'far al-Sadiq. The sixth Imam of the Shia school of thought, who had nearly 4,000 students attending his classes.

Like the other Imams from Ahlul Bayt, Imam al-Sadiq was put under house arrest and later imprisoned. Only after methods of intimidation and coercion to halt the spread of his teachings failed, did the Abbasid attempt to counter his ideas by creating another intellectual entity to

---

[32] *Al-Imamah wal-Siyasah*, 2:150

compete with him, in this case, the promotion of the Hanafi and Maliki schools of thought.

As it is said, people tend to follow the religion of their leaders;[33] therefore, the ideological path that the Abbasid government was laying out was rudimentary for the people to follow. Still, like the rest of the imams of Ahlul Bayt, Imam al-Sadiq gave up his life at the hands of the ruling power for his unwavering resistance to compromise the principles of Islam.

Shafi'i School of Thought (*Al-Madhab al-Shafi'i*)

From the time of his childhood, Imam Muhammad b. Idris al-Shafi'i (150 - 206 AH) immersed himself in the ideas of Imam Malik. He was inspired deeply by him and nearly memorized *al-Muwatta*. Eventually he procured a letter of recommendation from the governor of Mecca to the governor of Madinah enabling him to meet with Imam Malik, whose status was very high in Madinah during the Abbasid time. There he became a student of Imam Malik until the death of Imam Malik about nine years later.

At that time, Imam Shafi'i fell into poverty and was obliged to return to Mecca.[34] There, some individuals concerned about his condition, appealed to the governor of Yemen to find him an official position, and thus Imam al-Shafi'i was made the governor of the state of Najran in Yemen.

However, during the rule of Harun al-Rashid, Imam al-Shafi'i was accused of leaning towards the Alawiyin[35] and the school of Ahlul Bayt, and so he was brought to Baghdad, handcuffed. While he was being held as a prisoner, one of his friends, Muhammad b. al-Hasan al-Shaybani (who was also one of the primary advocates of the Hanafi school of thought for the Abbasid) interceded on his behalf and testified that al-

---

[33] *Al-Nas ala Deen Mulukihim*

[34] *Mujam al-Udaba*, 17:287

[35] The descendants of the Holy Prophet through Imam Ali.

Shafi'i was not on the side of Ahlul Bayt and was completely supportive of the Abbasid government. This testimony resulted in the release of al-Shafi'i, and as a result, he became very close to al-Shaybani and studied under him, learning the opinions (*araa*) of Abu Hanifah in *ra'i* (opinion) and *qiyas* (analogy), both of which Abu Hanifah was well known for. However, the two differed regarding Ahlul Bayt - al-Shafi'i was in fact sympathetic towards their cause, while al-Shaybani was not.[36]

Out of these two influences: the Maliki school (which can also be referred to as the school of *athar* (text)) and the Hanafi school, was born the Shafi'i school of thought. In 199 AH, Imam al-Shafi'i moved to Egypt along with Ibn Abdullah al-Abbas, the governor of Egypt. There, his school slowly began to spread. Unfortunately, because he differed on some points with Imam Malik, Imam al-Shafi'i incurred the anger of many of the adherents of the Maliki school in Egypt, and they eventually rioted and killed him.

It is worth noting that al-Bukhari and al-Muslim did not narrate any hadith from al-Shafi'i - not because he was inferior in knowledge, but because he had inclinations towards the school of Ahlul Bayt. He said that Ali b. Ali Talib had the right to leadership at the time over Mu'awiyah and his companions,[37] who were the group that began the assault on Islam. He displayed love for Ahlul Bayt and the family of the Prophet and proclaimed, "If anyone who loves the Ahlul Bayt is a *rafidi* (a rejecter of the three caliphates) then let the whole world witness that I am the first *rafidi*." Such statements not only led to his arrest as mentioned before, but also resulted in silencing his books of hadith.

Hanbali School of Thought (*Al-Madhab al-Hanbali*)

Imam Ahmad b. Hanbal (165 - 240 AH) was born in Baghdad. At the age of fifteen, he embarked on journeys to different countries to meet with various scholars. While in Baghdad, he studied under Imam al-Shafi'i,

---

[36] *Tarikh Baghdad*, 2:178

[37] *Ali b. Abi Talib huwa al-Imam al-Haq.*

who inspired him considerably, and Abu Yusuf al-Qadi. At the time, there were two competing schools: *madrasah al-athar* (the school focusing on texts) and *madrasah al-ra'i wal-qiyas* (the school based on opinion and analogy), and Ibn Hanbal favored the former.

Although like other scholars, he too relocated to Hijaz, however he was not as well known as the leaders of the other schools of thought because most considered him to be a *muhaddith* (narrator of hadith) instead of a genuine *faqih* (jurist).

Ibn Hanbal was a strong advocate of the Abbasid government and when al-Mutawakil came to power in 232 AH, he tortured the Alawiyin and fiercely opposed the school of Ahlul Bayt, but he paid Ibn Hanbal a handsome salary of 4,000 *dirhams,* and invited him to Samarra to obtain blessings from his presence.[38]

Ahmad b. al-Hanbal wrote his famous work *Musnad Ahmad b. Hanbal* under the reign of al-Mutawakil and passed away while al-Mutawakil was still in power. His case was similar to that of Imam al-Malik, whose ideas were also propagated by the Abbasid caliphate, and the Abbasid promoted both of their schools of thought.

---

[38] *Al-Bidayah wal-Nihayah,* 10:350

Conclusion

A fundamental principle of the Muslims is that Islam has been perfected by God, "This day I have perfected your religion for you, completed My favor upon you, and have chosen for you Islam as your religion." (c. 5:3)

Muslims also consider Prophet Muhammad as the best example to emulate, "Verily, in the Apostle of God you have a good example [to follow] for everyone who looks forward [with hope and awe] to God and the Last Day, and remembers God unceasingly." (c. 33:21)

Having believed in these two proclamations, those who held the highest office of authority in Islam - the caliphate (from after the Prophet's death until the collapse of the caliphate rule in 1923) - should have been more attentive to preserve and protect the integrity of Islam and follow the ways of Prophet Muhammad without any modifications, alterations, innovations, or introduction of new practices. However, this was not the case, as mentioned throughout this book.

Some people continue to argue that "the Shia are the innovators of Islam," and that it is actually the Shia who have introduced new ideas and concepts into Islam, when in fact, through careful research and examination of Islamic history and jurisprudence this accusation becomes baseless.

Even as recently as in 2008, a well-known Egyptian cleric (considered as a "moderate" figure) reiterated the same propaganda, which caused a wave of rebuttals from Shia scholars. In part, this book is a reply to such accusations and labeling as well.

Although, the thought of writing this book came about some ten years ago, the writing took an intermission of six of those years; and what urged its publication now are the false accusations being hurled against the followers of Ahlul Bayt, which extensively arise from global pulpits and through multi-media sources. My conscience did not permit me to remain on the sideline and be silent about this matter any longer.

The truth of the matter is, and as this book details, the innovations and alterations were never started or practiced by the followers of Ahlul Bayt; rather, the Shia have always maintained, without waiver or variation that they follow the path of the Prophet.

In part, in our times we are witnessing the effect of the past on the present. Today's violent acts of terrorism and the radical ideological interpretation being perpetrated by some "Muslims" against Muslims and non-Muslims are conjoined to the times of the early Muslim governance and their successive caliphate regimes. The Muslim leaders of the past, like those of the Umayyah and Abbasid dynasties, mentally and culturally cultivated the seeds of anarchic dogma, hatred, and violence, which is present among the most extremist Muslim parties of today. Establishments like the Taliban and the teachings of the Wahhabis are deeply rooted in the same radical mentality and hegemonic control like the ones of the past.

Our time has witnessed people like Abu Musab al-Zarqawi, the sinister aid of al-Qaida who introduced suicide bombers to the streets of Iraq and caused thousands of lives to be lost. We can also see this totalitarian and violent force on the streets of Kabul, Mumbai, Jakarta, and Islamabad, and on the dreadful day of 9-11-2001.

It is the anticipation of the author of this book, for the reader to know the reality. As a scholar and researcher it is incumbent to ascend personal interest and contracted thoughts, and to speak the rightful truth without apprehension. I am held to the highest degree by the covenant taken from the early scholars by which Allah holds them to the following, "Those who conceal the clear (Signs) We have sent down, and the Guidance, after We have made it clear for the people in the Book, on them shall be Allah's curse, and the curse of those entitled to curse." (c. 2:159) Along with, "And remember Allah took a covenant from the People of the Book, to make it known and clear to mankind, and not to hide it; but they threw it away behind their backs, and purchased with it some miserable gain! And vile was the bargain that they made!" (c. 3:187)

What has been documented and cited in this work are facts, written by the most revered authentic (*sahih*) books and respected Sunni scholars. Thus, no one can argue that the author was relying on outside sources; and in addition, not one source has been taken out of context or exaggerated.

Some may argue that there is no need to frequent the past of the Muslims. As difficult as it may be, the past of the Muslims should not be impervious. Muslims must know their history in order to understand the current predicament they find themselves in. There are reasons why the state of the ummah is the way it is today. The record shows that in our history there were certain Muslims who affected the course of Islam and Muslims forever - politically, theologically, and historically.

The Quraysh group had systematically planned, influenced, and executed the orders of the caliph and wished to design it as a revolving political hegemony. Even on the deathbed of the Prophet, they prevented the Prophet from writing his will - a will that would have forever guarded the ummah from misguidance - and then they sealed it at Saqifah. In the words of the second caliph himself, they prevented the Prophet from writing his will because they did not want both prophethood and successorship vested in Bani Hashim, namely Ali b. Abi Talib. In short, the pre-Islamic Arab rivalry first impregnated the division of the ummah.

Shia and Sunni have two opposing views when it comes to the appointment of the caliph. According to the Ahlul Bayt, Allah ordains the highest accolade (leadership office) of the ummah. On the other end, the Sunni believe that it is one of consulate (*shura*). Although, the early history of political Islam records that "*shura*" was never fairly executed, nor was the method of it consistent as seen in the appointments of the first three caliphs and the caliphs of the Umayyad and Abbasid dynasties.

To leave the ummah without continued Divine guidance would be to expose the religion to unwarranted innovations, modifications, and personal conjecture.

149

The history of the Islamic caliphate earmarks acts of nepotism, corruption, and incompetency, primarily witnessed during the reins of Uthman, Bani Umayyah, and Bani Abbas. We find unqualified and incompetent leaders who changed and modified Islam, and practiced nepotism and favoritism.

One day, a group of companions was with the Prophet and they said, "O Allah's Apostle! We know how to greet you, but how should we invoke Allah for you?" The Prophet said, "Say: 'O Allah! Send your blessings (greeting, which is God's mercy upon the Prophet - *salawat*) on Muhammad and his family, the same way as You sent Your blessings (greetings & mercy) on Ibrahim's family; You are indeed worthy of all praise, full of glory.'"[1] On another occasion, the Prophet said to his companions, "Do not salute me in short!" The companions asked, "What is saluting you in short?" The Prophet replied, "Saying that blessing (mercy) of Allah be upon Muhammad." They asked, "What should we say?" The Prophet answered, "Say: 'Blessing (mercy) of Allah be upon Muhammad and his Ahlul Bayt!'"[2] Despite being purified by Allah (c. 33:33) and recognized by the Prophet, a misfortunate mistreatment of the household of the Prophet by some of the companions has been recorded in history. The attempt to burn the house of Fatima and Ali, denying them economic power by confiscating their property, and a forty-year campaign to smear and discredit them are just some of the ill workings made by those who stood to secure their power post and sway public opinion against the household of the Prophet.

Most notably, one of the most consequential effects on the ummah was depriving them of the unabridged sayings (Hadith) of the Prophet. The Prophet emphatically urged his companions to write his sayings, but unfortunately, those who held power prevented this writing, and even barred those from traveling so as to not inform others about the Prophet's sayings. Eventually, unsubstantiated hadith surfaced - even

---

[1] Ibn Hajar, *Al-Sawa'iq al-Muhriqah*, c.11, section 1, p.225

[2] *Sahih al-Bukhari*, 6.320

ludicrous ones - such as the hadith that exhorts the religious knowledge of the second caliph as being superior to that of the Prophet, or the Prophet frolicking with unveiled women! As a result, Muslim scholars had to develop the Science of Hadith, in which each hadith went under intense scrutiny to ascertain its authenticity.

Although the followers of Ahlul Bayt continued to record the hadith and passed them along to their followers, nonetheless they were the minority as opposed to the majority who held public attitude. The trepidation of transmitting the hadith was a form of maintaining dominance of the caliphate, because had the hadith about the Ahlul Bayt (especially the Prophet's appointment of Ali b. Abi Talib as his successor and the importance of adhering to his family on numerous occasions) circulated, then the ummah would have known the truth. The consequence is that the people would have instigated a collapse of the illegitimate institute of the caliphate and those appointed.

Understanding that the historical and political aspects covered throughout this book may be delicate for some; nonetheless, never is it meant to be as a means to jostle sectarian division - this is far from my intention. I have maintained judicious care in the manner of presenting this work, but it is my belief that in order for Islam and Muslims to go forward in harmony and solidarity, we have to have the courage to recognize the truth of our past and rationally discuss the matter in a dignified and scholarly fashion.

When an injustice is done in the past against others, then it becomes incumbent upon the people of the present to acknowledge it and make amends. This needs to happen so that the Muslims can truly practice what Allah has intended for them - a religion of brotherhood, peace, and justice.

Until the end of time, even the most sincere Muslims will disagree upon what they truly believe is the most correct path. However, while accepting that there will be disagreement, it is important to represent each school of thought accurately - as it represents itself, and as reliable and mutually agreed-upon historical sources represents it, rather than continue to propagate confusion.

I do not believe that the divisions amongst the Muslims are an irreparable part of our history. If Muslims and non-Muslims can sit side by side, have intellectual and scholarly discussions, engage in a deeper understanding about each other's faith, and then publish their findings, then what prevents responsible and respected Shia and Sunni Muslim scholars from doing the same? The time has come to hold such dialogue.

I continue to uphold and encourage an open and rational discussion policy with my colleagues. The invitation to hold such roundtable discussions remains open and is welcomed. ❀

Glossary

A

Aam: general

Abdullah: slave or servant of Allah

Abi (abi): father of...

Adalah: justice or integrity

Adhan: Muslim call to prayer

Ajr: reward

Ambiya: prophets

Ameen: trustworthy

Amir: commander

Ara(a): opinion(s)

Asabiyah: bigotry (p.20)

Athar: text

Awla: has more authority (p.9)

Ayah: Qur'anic verse

B

Baatil: falsehood

Bayah: allegiance

Bayt al-mal: public treasury

Bidah: religious innovation

Bint: daughter of...

D

Diyyah: blood money

Durrah: stick

Deen: faith

Dinars: golden coin currency

Dirhams: silver coin currency

Dunyah: life

F

Faasiq: disbeliever

Fusuq: impiety

Fay: income for all of the Muslim community

Fuqaha: jurists

G

Ghazw: military dispatch

Ghina: singing

H

Hadi: guide

Hadith: practice and saying of the Holy Prophet

Hijab: covering for a Muslim woman

Hijrah: migration (there are two known Muslim hijrah: lesser hijrah; was when a small group (70 Muslims) escaped from Mecca to Ethiopia, and the most famous was, the migration from Mecca to Madinah by the Prophet and his followers)

Hijrah: Islamic lunar calendar – and also defined as: the start of the Islamic year

Huffaz: narrators

Hujjaj: pilgrims

I

Ibn (b.): son of ...

Ifta: giving religious edict

Ihdath: a new innovation

Ijtihad: deducing Muslim law

Imamah: leadership

Intahayna: stopped

Iqamah: refers to the second call for the prayer that follows the first call (adhan). It means that the prayer is ready to start

Isnad: chain of narrators

Itrati: my family

J

Jahiliyyah: ignorance (pre-Islamic era)

Janabah: ritual impurity

Jinn: spirits

K

Khass: specific

Khalifah: leader

Khazima: single evidence

Khilafat: leadership

Kisa: cloak

Kufr: apostasy

M

(al-)Madhab: school of Islamic thought

Mahdi: guided one

Masjid: mosque

Mawla: guardian, leader, or master

Minbar: pulpit

Muadhdhin: the person calling out the call to prayer (also called: *muezzin*)

Mubayan: clearly recognized

Mubahilah: invocation

Muhaddithun: narrators

Muhaddith: narrator of hadith

Muhkam: fundamental or basic

Munsukh: abrogated

Mujmal: unexplained

Mushnat: Jewish scripts

Mushrikeen (plural) (*mushrik*: singular): a person who associate someone or something with God)

Mutashabih: vague

N

Nabeeth: a form of wine

Nasikh: abrogating

Q

Qadha: judiciary leadership

(al-)Qada: judiciary system

Qasr: shortened version

Qayyid(u): document

Qayyim: self-subsisting

Qiyas: analogy

R

Rafidah: rejecters

Ra´i: opinion

Raja: return

Rakat(s): unit(s) of prayer

Riyasah: leadership

Rukhsah: leniency

S

Sadaq: truthful

Sahaabah: companions

Shadaid: harshness

Shaheed: witness

Sharia: law

Shaytan: Satan

Shawath: eccentricity

Siddiq: truthful person

Surah: chapter of the Qur'an

Shura: consultation

T

Tabieen: second generation after the *sahabahs*

Tafseer: the interpretation or explanation of the verses of the Holy Qur'an or hadith

Taharah: ritual Purity

Takbeer: uttering "Allahu akbar"

Tayammum: ritual purification by means of dust

U

Ummah: Muslim nation

Usuliyun: jurists of Islamic law

Uktub(u): write

W

Wilayah: Authority

Wudhu: ablution for prayer

Y

Yahjor: hallucination

Index